The Function of Ideals and Attitudes in Social Education

AN EXPERIMENTAL STUDY

BY

Paul Frederick Voelker, Ph.D.
President of Olivet College
Olivet, Michigan

TEACHERS COLLEGE, COLUMBIA UNIVERSITY
CONTRIBUTIONS TO EDUCATION, NO. 112

Published by
Teachers College, Columbia University
NEW YORK CITY
1921

COPYRIGHT, 1921, BY PAUL F. VOELKER

ACKNOWLEDGMENTS

AN experimental study such as is described in this volume could not be successfully accomplished by one person alone. Many individuals and groups of individuals have contributed directly or indirectly to this investigation. It will not be possible to make full acknowledgment of my indebtedness to all those who have assisted; I shall therefore merely mention the names of those who were most directly concerned with the success of the undertaking.

Professor William C. Bagley, because of his unwavering faith in the function of ideals as agencies in the control of conduct, was my constant source of inspiration. Professor E. L. Thorndike's brilliant genius was the guide in all of the experimental work. Professor David Snedden's stimulating criticisms helped to keep my study within practical bounds. Professor H. A. Ruger placed all the facilities of his laboratory at my disposal. Professors Thomas H. Briggs, William H. Kilpatrick, Truman L. Kelley, E. K. Fretwell, Dr. I. L. Kandel, and Deans James E. Russell and Frederick J. E. Woodbridge gave valuable suggestions. The officers of Bryson Library, especially Miss Ethel Richmond and Miss Margaret Miller, rendered many special favors. My assistants in the experiment, Miss Gladys Fairbanks, Miss May Bere, Miss Grace Taylor, and Mr. M. E. Little, were of inestimable service.

Special mention is due to The Interchurch World Movement of North America, and to several of its officers, Mr. J. T. Giles, Professor Walter S. Athearn, and Dr. A. D. Yocum, for valuable cooperation; also to the Boy Scouts of America, and several of its officers, among them Mr. James E. West, Dr. W. H. Hurt, Mr. Myron Geddes, Mr. Wallace L. Neill, and Mr. C. A. Edson.

Several commercial concerns rendered valuable help. Among them are the Richard Hudnut Company, through its president, Mr. G. A. Pfeiffer; the Hammersley Manufacturing Company, and W. H. Thompson and Company.

Last, but not least, I acknowledge the devoted and untiring assistance rendered by my wife.

PAUL F. VOELKER

CONTENTS

CHAPTER I. The Perspective 1

CHAPTER II. The Problem of the Objectives of Social Education 5

CHAPTER III. The Problem of Methods 29

CHAPTER IV. The Problem of the Function of Ideals and Attitudes 42

CHAPTER V. An Experiment 57

CHAPTER VI. Conclusions 120

CHAPTER I

THE PERSPECTIVE

Social education is a business of prime importance to the life of a democracy. The adequate accomplishment of this business is an essential condition under which democracy can be realized: it is a fundamental prerequisite to the ends for which popular government was established; and it is a necessary preventive of certain social defects which tend to develop under the operation of *laissez-faire* institutions. From the standpoint of the individual, social education is the preparation for participation in group life; from the standpoint of society it is the training of the group in the collective performance of the functions of its community life. The individual must be taught to consider the social bearing of his conduct, he must be trained in the suppression of his anti-social impulses, and he must be socially motivated. The group as a whole must be made socially conscious, it must be taught to consider the effect of its collective conduct upon its individual members and upon the general welfare, and it must acquire the ability to act co-operatively in the protection of its community interests and in the conscious direction of its own progress.

It is only when viewed from the standpoint of society as a whole that the transcendent importance of social education in a democracy becomes apparent. Just as adaptation to his environment is an essential condition of the survival and prosperity of the individual, so is group adjustment to the exigencies of new situations a necessary condition of the progress and survival of the group. The very essence of democracy is collective action. If collective action is to be in the interests of the general welfare, if it is to tend toward social preservation and progress, it must be directed by intelligence and based upon justice. Social education will demand, therefore, not only the dissemination of information, but also the development of a sense of social solidarity, the cultivation of a keen sensitiveness to the encroachment of private interest upon the interests of the social body, the strengthening of social coherence to the point where public opinion can be utilized in the protection of community interests and in the conscious assistance of its own evolution. Modern society has become so highly articulated that "the welfare of all is at the mercy of each." In a mutualistic age such as ours, many of our vital interests must be entrusted to others. The greatest danger to individual and social welfare comes from the betrayal of trust. It is the business of organized society to protect itself and its weaker members from betrayal at the hands of those who are both strong and selfish. This can be done by a process of social education which will make the individual more trustworthy and which will make society more efficient in its collective functions. Democratic institutions of themselves are not effective. Each generation must work out its own salvation by mastering the use of the instrumentalities upon which freedom, justice, and progress depend. If the training of future citizens in the use of these instrumentalities is left to chance, each succeeding generation will drift with the current of its own times. If it is neglected, popular government will be in danger of destruction by the very individualism which democracy has set free.

It is a curious fact, however, that while the importance of social education is universally admitted in theory, in the actual practice of our schools it does not receive the emphasis which it deserves. It is true that from the beginning of our public school systems in America, the general aim of education has been preparation for citizenship. At least this has been the implied aim; this has been the reason for levying taxes for the support of public schools. But this general aim has gradually been subverted into the more individualistic aims of imparting cultural knowledge or of developing vocational skill as a means of giving advantage to individuals in their struggle for existence. To-day the avowed purpose of the schools is service in the interests of individuals, their method is utilization of individual effort, and the motive to which they most frequently appeal is individual success. Individual efficiency is the primary product; social efficiency is the by-product of our educational systems. Whatever social efficiency we have achieved has depended largely upon accidental influences, such as the personality of the teacher, the traditions of the playground, and the informal education of the home, the church, the neighborhood, and the street. The net result of our formal education has been enlightened self-interest; social motivation has been neglected. We have given little attention to the development of group loyalty, initiative, and co-operation, which are the raw materials out of which good citizenship is made. The result has been that the more efficient our schools have become as individualizing agencies, the more have they tended to weaken the social order which they were organized to perpetuate. Many of our present problems are probably the actual result of our individualistic education.

One chief reason for this state of affairs is that America has not yet developed a national program of education. Until such a program is provided, it will be impossible to achieve definite results in social education on a nation-wide scale. The time has come for the educators in this country to work out such a program. They must determine what should be done, how the desired results are to be obtained, and how these results will fit into the American democratic scheme of things. Education is becoming conscious of its social mission and purpose. It will need to shake off the inertia of our long-established systems which have become entirely unequal to the accomplishment of the task imposed upon them by the complex industrial conditions of the twentieth century. It will need to provide for the situation produced by the increasing density and heterogeneity of our population. It will need to adjust itself "to certain fundamental changes in social insight . . . [which] tend to nullify the effectiveness of the historic means of social control . . . the motive power of which was authority." (David Snedden, in *The International Journal of Ethics*, Vol. XXX, No. 1.) It will need to sever connection with the point of view of the political philosophers of the nineteenth century, who preached the gospel of the rights of the individual, and to proclaim a twentieth-century gospel of the rights of the community and the duties of the individual, even to the extent of taking away from the individual some of the liberties which in a former generation would have been considered inalienable. Our educational program will need to consider, not only the efficiency and happiness of the individual, but the efficiency and the welfare of the entire social body.

The general aim of this study, therefore, is to try to find a secure basis upon which a broad program of social education may be built. Its specific aims are first, to determine what are a few of the more important objectives of social education upon which there may be general agreement; second, to assemble and interpret certain widely approved and understood methods of teaching; and third, to investigate whether certain moral, civic, and religious standards of behavior, inculcated by certain methods of teaching, will actually serve in the guidance and control of conduct.

CHAPTER II

THE PROBLEM OF THE OBJECTIVES OF SOCIAL EDUCATION

The first problem to be solved before an adequate program of social education can be planned is the formulation of definite objectives in terms of social values. It is not the purpose of this study to solve this problem, but only to point out its importance, and to forecast what seems to be a reasonable solution.

It will be necessary for us to know what the product of social education should be before we can intelligently produce it. The qualities of citizenship are not mysterious qualities which we somehow acquire. They must be intelligently aimed at and striven for. It is hardly living up to our responsibilities as educators to point out that the boys and girls of our schools are in the main on the road to good citizenship without any effort on our part. If this can be shown to be true, it is part of the business of educators to ascertain what agencies are putting them on the road to good citizenship, and to supplement the work of these agencies if their efforts are deficient in any direction. Anything less is a shirking of responsibility on the part of those to whom the work of training our future citizens is entrusted. It is the business of the direct educational agencies of the nation to define the aims of social education, to provide for measuring the achievement of results from whatever indirect influences, and to supply whatever deficiencies may be revealed.

There are certain qualities of citizenship which may be called the irreducible minimum. These qualities will be demanded of every citizen, no matter what his station in life, no matter what his degree of native ability. It is evident that if these qualities be set up as objectives of social education, they will need to be defined in terms rather general, yet sufficiently simple to be understood by the humblest teacher of the land, and sufficiently flexible to permit of their adjustment to peculiar local and individual needs. It is also evident that these basic objectives of social education should all be within reach during the first six years of school life, for the reason that the majority of our future citizens do not continue their school work beyond that period. It would be a physical impossibility to mention all the specific objectives that would be desirable for every individual and group of individuals, and such a list would not be useful to the majority. A national program of social education can be built up only with large general objectives in view—objectives which will include the virtues that are fundamental to moral conduct, social efficiency, and good citizenship in a democracy. If our social objectives cannot be expressed in broad terms, it will be impossible to build a single national program; we would need as many programs as there are clearly defined groups within the social body.

It seems reasonable, therefore, that the aims of social education should be expressed in terms of ideals and attitudes. "To transmit worthy ideals from generation to generation is the prime task of education." (Bagley: *Educational Values*, p. 45.) This does not mean that there are not many specific responses required in moral conduct and in good citizenship. On the contrary, it means that many such specific responses will be included under these general objectives, each specific response having a common element which unites it with other specific responses under a general rubric. This common element may be one of content, of method, or of purpose. (See Ruediger, in *Educational Review*, Vol. 36, 1908, p. 364.) In social education, the element of purpose may be of greater importance than either of the others. For example, the future bricklayer, porter, shoemaker, judge, and physician would receive little common information that would assist each of them in making the proper social responses in the discharge of his respective duties. Nor would there be many common elements in the method by which they had learned, or in which they performed their respective duties. However, there would be many identical elements of purpose: the purpose to be of service to their community and to their fellow-men; the purpose to render value for the compensation which they receive; the purpose to co-operate with others; the purpose to be worthy of the trust of their fellows; the purpose to work for the general welfare. Each individual could be dominated by the same general purpose and yet react to a given situation in his own specific way.

There are positive advantages in stating the objectives of social education in large terms rather than in narrow terms, provided they can be clearly defined. First of all, by this means the entire list of objectives can be stated in a few words, and a wider interest in and acceptance of the program will be more likely. In the second place, desirable ideals and attitudes can be handled in bundles, as it were, and many related specific objectives can be subsumed and developed under each. If an entire school, for example, were to accept the ideal of social service, and if a spirit of mutual helpfulness were created in that school, every individual who absorbed that spirit could be swayed by a number of specific social motives that are closely related to the social service ideal. A boy devoted to the social service of his fellows would be less likely to steal from them, to lie about them, to be deceitful to them, or to be disloyal to them. He would be more likely to feel a sense of responsibility toward them, to feel sympathy toward them, to exercise a certain amount of initiative in service to them. It would be more difficult for him to be unfair to any member of the group if he were animated by the ideal of service to them all. Thus the entire scheme of social education could be bound up within a dozen ideals and attitudes, and could be made so simple that even the inexperienced teacher would be able to profit by it. Further, this plan would enable education to build upon the gregarious instincts instead of trying to root them out. Gang loyalty is the foundation upon which the larger loyalties may be built. It should be regarded as a potential virtue rather than as a vice. It should be directed, and not destroyed. However, the usual method of procedure in attempting to teach school or civic loyalty is to combat those smaller loyalties which may not be immediately beneficial to the larger loyalty, and which may in fact be temporarily inimical. A better method of procedure will be to strengthen the instinctive gang loyalty and to tie it to the ideal of loyalty, where it may serve to strengthen, not only loyalty to the gang, but also loyalty to the home, to the school, to the community, and to society at large.

If social education is to be of service in the conservation and improvement of our social order, it must set up general standards to which all individuals must be taught to conform. "The kind of education needed is the kind that breeds idealism among all classes of people. . . . Democracy cannot succeed where the people are selfish and interested alone in their own private good." (McGiffert, in *Religious Education*, Vol. XIV, pp. 157-58.) Democratic societies are forms of human will. They represent a purpose that demands the subordination, or socialization, of individual aims. If all members of a group acted in accordance with their spontaneous individual desires, group life would not be possible. Even a group of criminals imposes its law upon each individual member. In the ideal democracy which is to come, each individual will employ his talents in the service of the common weal, because the service of the group will be his own service, the interests of the group will be his own interests, and the will of the group will be his own will. The democracy which is to come will be a creature of evolution, not revolution. It will be a thing of education, a being in the minds of men, expressive of common ideals, motivated by common purposes, and stabilized by common attitudes.

One of the most widely accepted statements of the objectives of social education in this country is the one prepared for the Boy Scouts of America. It is known as the Scout Oath and Law. Its twelve objectives are expressed in terms of ideals and attitudes, so defined and described that they can easily be understood and obeyed. The fact that they are accepted by a large number of volunteer workers and obeyed by thousands of young Americans makes these ideals worthy of the attention of everyone interested in the problems of social education. Another important statement of objectives is known as The Children's Code of Morals, prepared by Professor William Hutchins for the National Institution for Moral Instruction. Other attempts have been made, nearly all of them heading in the same direction.

It is not with the purpose of discrediting any of the attempts that have been made, but rather of supplementing them that the following objectives are proposed. They have been compiled from many sources and are a composite of many judgments. Some of them overlap, but this difficulty cannot easily be avoided. All reference to intellectual and vocational objectives has been omitted, not because these are to be overlooked, but because they are here considered to be of secondary importance—as tools rather than as ends in the affairs of life, and as deriving their chief value from the relations which they sustain to the objectives of social education.

There is perhaps no one social ideal which transcends all of the others in importance. All of them are to be kept in view and consciously striven for if the forces of education are to evolve a more and more nearly perfect social order. Moreover, the inculcation of any high ideal will probably be of service in the inculcation of other ideals. It is hardly conceivable that a boy could be made sympathetic without at the same time being made more tolerant; that he could be trained in loyalty without learning something of co-operation. All of the group virtues or ideals that are here proposed have a tendency to dovetail with some of the other virtues or ideals, and any method of training which may prove to be effective, could not be limited in its results to the strengthening of one ideal alone.

The Ideal of Trustworthiness

The first ideal or objective of social education which is proposed is the ideal of trustworthiness. There are two reasons for placing it at the beginning of the list: first, because it is outside the realm of controversy—the most extreme individualist and proponent of *laissez-faire* conditions will demand trustworthiness no less than the extremest communist who would destroy every vestige of individuality; and second, because trustworthiness is at the very heart of the Scouting movement, which is the most widely organized attempt to inculcate civic ideals that this country has ever known. The first law of the scout is trustworthiness. The scout vows "to do his best to do his duty to God and his country; to obey the Scout law; to help other people at all times; and to keep himself physically strong, mentally awake, and morally straight." Having taken the Scout Oath, he is placed on his honor, and in all of his future relationships he is made more or less conscious that he is expected to be worthy of trust. Trustworthiness, therefore, is at the very heart of the Scout's ideals.

The same ideal is expressed in the fourth law, the Law of Reliability, of the Children's Code of Morals, as follows:

The good American is reliable. Our country grows great and good as her citizens are able more fully to trust each other. *Therefore:*

1. I will be honest in word and in act. I will not lie, sneak, or pretend, nor will I keep the truth from those who have a right to it.
2. I will not do wrong in the hope of not being found out. I cannot hide the truth from myself, and cannot often hide it from others.
3. I will not take without permission what does not belong to me.
4. I will do promptly what I have promised to do. If I have made a foolish promise I will at once confess my mistake, and I will try to make good any harm which my mistake may have caused. I will so speak and act that people will find it easier to trust each other.

While it is impossible to anticipate all of the situations in the active life of an adult citizen in which the ideal of trustworthiness may be expected to determine conduct, it is possible to define a number of school situations in which trustworthiness is essential. This has been done admirably, not only for trustworthiness, but for many of the other essential qualities of good citizenship, by Siegried Maia Upton and Clara Frances Chassell, in an article entitled, "A Scale for Measuring the Importance of Habits of Good Citizenship," and published in the *Teachers College Record*, Vol. XX, No. 1. An enumeration of these will serve as a concrete and suggestive, if not a comprehensive definition of the ideal itself. If an individual is trustworthy, he can be trusted to make the proper response when confronted with the following situations:

1. To do a given task exactly as it was given to him to do;
2. To work as faithfully when he works alone as when observed;
3. To stick to a point when he knows he is right;
4. To avoid taking property belonging to others;
5. To avoid making false claims about himself;
6. To be fair in an examination or in a test;
7. To return borrowed money or other borrowed property;
8. To keep a promise or other agreement;
9. To repeat a message as it was given to him to repeat;
10. To keep a secret if he agreed to do so;
11. To be honest when he scores his own record;
12. To perform an errand without loitering on the way;
13. To try to return a lost article to its owner;
14. To refuse to accept change given to him by mistake;
15. To perform an errand, or render any other service, when no one will ever know whether he did;
16. To play in a game without cheating.

Mr. Charles M. Schwab, in a recent address to the undergraduates of Princeton University, outlining what he conceives to be the fundamental requirements for a successful life, places "unimpeachable integrity" at the head of the list. He has chosen simply another term for trustworthiness. Even if his definition of a successful life is entirely individualistic, the social value of trustworthiness is truly estimated. No individual is worthy of group membership until he is trustworthy. The sense of responsibility is the balance to freedom. No one is really trustworthy until he has the welfare of the entire social body at heart; until he would as soon deceive himself, cheat himself, steal from himself as to commit these offences against others or against the group. The really trustworthy individual feels a sense of responsibility for the welfare of the entire group to which he belongs and strives for the successful performance of the duties that are assigned to him.

It requires no argument to prove that no country would be fit to live in if its citizens were unable to trust one another. The foundations of industrial, social, and political life require mutual confidence and trust. In its negative sense trustworthiness means a reaction against lying, pretending, deceiving, cheating, stealing, breaking promises or taking selfish advantage of others. In its positive sense it includes a willingness to accept legitimate responsibility in group affairs; the desire to do good and thorough work in whatever position one is placed; promptness in the fulfillment of one's obligations; self-reliance in the performance of one's duties; and a sincere feeling of obligation to keep one's word or faith toward any individual with whom one is in direct relationship, or toward the entire group which is concerned with one's action.

Considered as a broad objective of social education in a democracy, trustworthiness is an ideal of transcendent importance. Under an autocratic government, each subject of the empire is responsible to the autocrat. Under a democratic government, each citizen is responsible to the social group. It may be that our schools have not achieved the best possible results in social education because they have not held up the ideal of social responsibility. The students are usually held responsible to the individual teacher. In order to make them trustworthy citizens, they should be held responsible to the social group to which they belong. The boy should be taught to be responsible to his gang, and the girl to her class or set. Each individual should be made to feel that some certain work belongs to him to do, that a certain kind of conduct is expected of him, and that a certain contribution to the general welfare is demanded of him. He must be made to feel that the group is depending upon him, and that all the plans of the group will fail if he fails to do his part. If a responsibility is placed upon an individual member of a group, he should be held accountable, not to any teacher or other authority outside of the group, but to the organized opinion of his own peers. If each individual in the group accepts this ideal of social responsibility, and if each group is trained in holding its individual members accountable to the will of the organization, the citizens of our future democracy will be a step in advance of the present generation, in their possession of a stronger spirit of mutual trust.

OTHER OBJECTIVES OF SOCIAL EDUCATION

No attempt will be made in this discussion to demonstrate the need or the function of all of the ideals or objectives of social education that are herein suggested. Nor will the enumeration necessarily be exhaustive. It seems desirable, however, to mention and briefly discuss a few of the seemingly more important ones for the sake of giving the general perspective out of which the main problem has grown, and of pointing out the possible applications if the main problem can be solved. If any one of these ideals can be taught by the methods herein proposed, and if its function in the control of conduct can be shown to be sufficiently important to warrant the expenditure of effort, then the inculcation of all the other ideals by means of similar methods may confidently be undertaken, and a broad program of social education may be planned with reasonable expectation of success.

LOYALTY

Considered as one of the broad objectives of social education, loyalty is something more than an instinct, and more than a habit. There is doubtless an instinctive tendency, closely allied to gregariousness and sociability, to be loyal to the group to which one belongs. This tendency manifests itself in the solidarity of the gang, in the coherence of the school when one of its members is attacked by an outsider or reprimanded by a teacher, and in war. Loyalty of this kind does not require training; it requires only opportunity for expression; for it is as fundamental as human nature. There is another kind of loyalty which lies in the realm of habit. Such loyalty is often developed in a laborer toward his employer, in a soldier toward his commander, in a student toward his teacher. Habitual loyalties are specific. They grow out of personal and business relationships. There are many such loyalties: to the family, to one's neighbors, friends, townsmen, and fraternal associates. These specific loyalties tend to spring up in any individual who is accepted and approved by other individuals or by a group, and they develop in strength if satisfactory relationships be long continued. They manifest themselves in the disposition to associate, in friendliness, in mutual service and affection. Most of these specific loyalties are characteristic of individual and small group relationships. Most of them tend to become exclusive responses, so that loyalty toward one's family group or business associates or fraternal organization often implies indifference or even hostility toward other individuals and toward other groups.

But there is a larger loyalty, a spirit, an ideal, an attitude, which, when properly defined, "is the fulfilment of the whole moral law." (Royce: *The Philosophy of Loyalty*, pp. 15-131.) "All . . . my more natural and . . . accidental loyalties will be controlled and unified by . . . the principle that whatever my cause, it ought to be such as to further, so far as in me lies, the cause of universal loyalty. . . . I must choose forms of loyal conduct which appeal to my own nature. . . . I shall serve causes such as my natural temperament and my social opportunities suggest to me. I shall choose friends whom I like; my family, my community, my country, will be served partly because I find it interesting to be loyal to them. . . . Nevertheless . . . my causes must form a system. They must constitute in their entirety a single cause, my life of loyalty." Unless this larger loyalty can be instilled into most of the individuals composing society many of the specific loyalties will have an anti-social bearing. Not only that, but the specific habits of loyalty in every individual, unless guided by a generalized loyalty, will sometimes fail to operate. Unless an employee holds to a general ideal and attitude of loyalty, his specific loyalty toward his employer will tend to give way at the first strain of disagreement. But if he has a generalized spirit of loyalty, minor disagreements will not produce a break in the relationship. During the World War many of the naturalized German citizens of this country, whose specific bonds of loyalty to Germany at the outbreak of the war were as strong as their specific loyalty to America, nevertheless gave themselves wholeheartedly to the service of America, because their generalized ideal and attitude of loyalty was thrown on the side of the country to which they owe allegiance now. A specific loyalty will operate only in the presence of a specific situation: a generalized loyalty, if, indeed, such a response can be proved to exist, may operate in a situation which is altogether novel.

If there is to be such a thing as a spirit of loyalty on the part of our citizens toward the commonwealth, this spirit must be cultivated as a general rather than as a specific loyalty. Some of the activities by means of which our loyalty is expressed must needs be specific—saluting the flag, rising at the singing of the national anthem, obedience to certain laws, and truthful statements to the tax assessor. But if there is to be general obedience to all the laws, even those toward which no specific reaction has become habitual; if there is to be loyalty toward all the officers of the government, whether they belong to one political camp or to another; if there is to be a spirit of devotion toward the entire social group, including all factions,—capital and labor, North and South, Jew and Gentile, White and Black; if individual welfare and small group jealousies are to be secondary to the larger interests of the entire social body, and if all of humanity is to be uplifted instead of only a small section of it; then a generalized loyalty to humanity, an ideal and an attitude of loyalty will need to be cultivated and made part of the moral fibre of every citizen. The development of such an attitude, grounded on the deep instinctive tendency of gregariousness, and made explicit in a generalized ideal, will tend to overcome the smaller loyalties whenever they are inimical to the welfare of the larger group. When a boy is asked to tell tales on his gang before this larger ideal of loyalty has been accepted by him, not only is he in danger of being made an outcast by his gang for his faithlessness, henceforth to be forever distrusted and placed on the defensive in his social relationships; but his whole moral character is threatened. If he yields to the temptation to be disloyal to his gang, he does violence to his instinctive tendencies, and he breaks the chain of his specific habit. More than that: if he yields, he forms a bond of being disloyal which may make the formation of a generalized ideal of loyalty far more difficult of accomplishment in the future.

The function of a generalized ideal of loyalty will be to harmonize all the smaller loyalties which to any individual have become habitual. A good citizen is loyal to all to whom loyalty is due. He severs relationships with those who in word or in deed are unworthy of his loyalty because of their open or secret disloyalty to the interests of his country or humanity. If any specific habit of loyalty is not in harmony with these larger interests, it will be broken or disregarded. In time of national danger, the loyal citizen will break the ties of home and business, will sever relations of friendship, and will sacrifice whatever is needed in order to live up to his ideal of loyalty, in the defense of the honor, the liberty, and the welfare of his country. He will manifest a spirit such as was manifested by the heroes who are described in "The Charge of the Light Brigade," the spirit of blind, blithe loyalty, giving his all in the service of the common good.

Social Service

The third broad objective of social education which is herewith proposed is social service. From the standpoint of society this ideal or attitude may be regarded as the ultimate criterion of good citizenship. The best citizen may be defined as the one who contributes the most to the community welfare, and the worst citizen as the one who contributes the least in proportion to his ability. Activities that are a public benefit are of positive value; those that confer no public benefit are of zero value; those that are an actual detriment to society are of negative value. The algebraic sum of any individual's contributions to the community welfare in positive, zero, and negative activities may well be the measure of his value as a citizen. Social service is not measured by its compensation in dollars and cents. It has economic value, but it does not necessarily have economic rewards. The safety and progress of society have always depended largely upon the uncompensated services of certain of its members.

The evolution of human society has been accomplished by means of two factors,—competition and mutual aid. (See Kropotkin: *Mutual Aid, a Factor in Evolution*.) While both of these factors doubtless have an equally powerful instinctive sanction, and both have probably been of equal importance in the unconscious evolution of the human race, the factor of competition is perhaps receiving the greater stress in the more recent and conscious development of our modern civilization. The ideal which has been held up to the youth of our land for the past century or more has been the ideal of personal success. The spirit of competition in modern life and in our educational institutions has become intense. The idols of our time are the successful fighters, not the successful servants. "The effect upon college men of the conspicuous triumphs of some of the great trusts has been to force them to think that the ideals held up by their instructors were unpractical." It is perhaps as natural to serve others as to help one's self; but when the world's greatest rewards are given in the competitive fields of activity, these fields will attract the ambitious youth. To the extent that the original tendencies of man are capable of modification, to that extent will man under our present educational system tend to grow in the direction of selfishness rather than in the direction of mutual aid. The strength of man's instinctive tendency to serve his fellow-men is demonstrated in the fact that in spite of all the forces which are operating to make man more competitive and more selfish, the world is full of examples of those who sacrifice their time, their energy, and their very lives in the service—often the uncompensated service—of their fellow-men.

If the ideal of social service be accepted as a worthy objective of social education, competition will not necessarily be eliminated. Competition could be continued, but instead of competing for our own selfish ends we could learn to compete in being unselfish.

Such competition would have all the joy of victory and none of the sting of defeat. The winners would merely win the distinction of having rendered the greatest service. The losers would still be winners, for they would have the consciousness of having contributed to the welfare of all.

The attitude of social service will include not only a general willingness to be helpful, but also actual industriousness, and the greatest possible participation in all the community activities that will contribute to the general welfare. One of the mottoes of the Boy Scouts is: "Do a good turn every day." It seems that no finer ideal could be set before the young manhood of America. It is inconceivable that young men who render willing, uncompensated service to other individuals or to the group to which they belong, could ever go very far astray in doing injury to the people whom they have served.

Social Sympathy

Sutherland, in his two-volume work, entitled *The Rise and Growth of the Moral Instinct*, says that sympathy is the most fundamental of all the social and moral emotions. Considered as an objective of social education, sympathy is something more than an emotion. It is the concept of the brotherhood of man, illuminated by a sympathetic imagination of how the other half lives, and "set" with the purpose of ameliorating their condition. The attitude of sympathy includes consideration of the rights of others, friendliness, sociability, and the desire to make one's self fit for their companionship. The exercise of sympathy stimulates the search for common interests and paves the way for breadth of understanding. If it becomes a ruling attitude, it lifts the individual above snobbery and race prejudice; it helps him to avoid fights and grudges; it helps to inhibit the tendency to gossip or to speak unkindly of others; it helps conquer his native selfishness in always wanting his own way; it will make for politeness and help overcome rudeness; it will prevent his putting other people to unnecessary trouble, whether they are working for him or with him; it will prevent his being cruel to human beings and even to animals, and will stimulate him to give help where help is most needed.

In America, where there are many different races, colors, and conditions of life, social sympathy is a necessary objective of social education. Without it we can never become one great homogeneous people. We must learn to realize, as a people, that we have common dangers, common opportunities and common triumphs. Realizing our common experiences, each one being able to imagine himself in the situation of the other, we may hope to strengthen the bonds of sympathy and understanding among the members of our great heterogeneous American group, and develop greater coherence and unity in our common life.

In his recent book, *A First Book of School Celebrations* (P.S. King & Son, Ltd., London), Dr. F. H. Hayward says: "Physical blindness is as nothing compared with the mental and moral blindness which separates class from class, sex from sex, creed from creed, nation from nation. Are men never to understand each other better than they do? Is hatred, tinged either with fear or contempt, and based on ignorance and chronic separation, to be the rule for another series of centuries? And are our educationists, under the pretext of safeguarding the religious convictions of this or that sect, or the political opinions of this or that party, to refuse to do their part in the task of making the country a place fit for human beings to live in? (pp. 14f.)

"In a recent American work, Morrison Swift's *Can Mankind Survive?* the thesis is maintained that men for centuries taught hatred under the guise of patriotism, reform, order, and religion, and have, for those same centuries, been reaping the fruit of this accursed teaching."

What the world needs is,—"a gracious spiritual cement, binding young years with old years as well as, at any given moment of time, binding rich and poor, male and female, rational and superstitious, conservative and revolutionary." There is no "gracious spiritual cement" like the attitude of kindness, sympathy, and brotherly love.

Social Conscience

To build in the American people the ideal of a social conscience is no small task for education to set itself. Our social body is so huge and so complex, and withal so incoherent. In a small and homogeneous group, conscience develops automatically. Certain forms of conduct are found not to be conducive to the community welfare, hence they are condemned; other forms of conduct are found to be conducive to the community welfare, hence they are approved. Thus there gradually grows up a body of knowledge, "known to all," of what is approved and what is disapproved by common consent. In a complex and loosely knit social organization such as ours, it is impossible for one member of the social body to know what the other member does. Often the conduct of one member does not affect the welfare or happiness of any of his immediate neighbors. Often the conduct of one member of society affects a large number of individuals, but affects each of them so slightly that the effect is not noticeable unless considered collectively. The keen individual conscience which was developed in a more primitive state of society will protect men against the primitive crimes of bodily violence and crude theft: but, as Ross points out in *Sin and Society*, our primitive consciences will not protect us against the newer forms of crime which are possible because of wholesale methods, because of impersonal contacts and the long-distance relationships made necessary by the complexities of modern civilization. Men who would not think of wronging an individual will sometimes wrong the public: the directors of a public utilities corporation who make unjust charges; the man who expectorates in a public place and thereby spreads disease; the careless train dispatcher who wrecks a train; the public official who sells his vote; the worker who produces a defective wheel and causes the death of hundreds; the newspaper man who prints a falsehood. Men who are keenly sensitive with respect to their moral obligations toward private individuals are sometimes extremely obtuse with respect to their obligations toward the general public.

The reason for this is obvious. The social conscience, like the individual conscience, is a thing of education, an ideal. Bagley defines it as that ideal which impels men to judge of actions in the light of the social significance of their acts. (*Educational Values*, pp. 107 ff.) The ideal of a social conscience will include public honesty, the state's faithfulness to its obligations, the duty to work for the general welfare, and the duty to the future. In proportion as the social conscience becomes keen, each individual will feel it his duty to become as intelligent as possible; he will also feel under obligation to give honest labor for his compensation. A keen public conscience will demand of each individual in society that he perform his just share of service. Every bit of such service adds to the sum total of the general welfare, and every shirker not only fails to contribute his share, but is actually subtracting from the sum total of the goods that have been produced for the general weal.

Social Co-operation

Co-operation is not only a beautiful moral ideal toward which to strive: under the stress of modern conditions it has become an economic necessity. One man cannot build a city or a railroad. "That each of us may have bread, men have sowed and reaped, have made plows and threshers, have built mills and mined coal, have made stoves and kept stores in friendly co-operation." (*The Children's Code of Morals.*) Each individual who contributes his share of productive work, avoiding waste and confusion, keeping a cheerful attitude toward his work and a courteous attitude toward his fellow-workers, and doing team work as best he can, adds by his efforts to the sum total of human happiness.

The ideal of co-operation will include the ideal of social integration, the sense of oneness in a great social unit, and the purpose to fit into the general scheme of things. It will include the ideal of truly representative government, in which all the people will have a co-operative interest. The man who possesses the spirit of co-operation will desire the success of the group rather than his own personal success. He will be willing to share in every co-operative undertaking. He will be animated by a social motive and will gladly make sacrifices for the common good.

America has not yet learned the lesson of *general* social co-operation. So far we have learned to co-operate only in small groups, except perhaps in time of national danger. Our labor unions and our closely knit corporations have learned to co-operate, but they do not include the entire community. Each group seems to consider all outsiders as legitimate prey for exploitation. Individualism could not be more selfish or competitive than small group co-operation, for it fails to regard the rights of the general public. During the war period there has been much profiteering, to the enrichment of a few and the detriment of the many. If the one hundred million people who are suffering at the hands of the profiteers were able to co-operate, profiteering would have to stop within twenty-four hours. Recently a Providence shoe firm was found guilty of profiteering in shoes to the extent of 800 per cent. "We have no defense to offer," was the firm's reply to the charges preferred by the district attorney. Said the Philadelphia *Public Ledger* in an editorial:

"Imagine American citizens making 800 per cent on an article of absolute necessity during a period when the intolerable rise in the cost of living is causing a wide-spread sense of deeply resented injustice throughout the country. Profiteering stalks as a national danger . . . . The hand of the law cannot be too heavy upon such practices. They are akin to treason in war time."

Co-operative stores have never flourished in America, in spite of the constant outcry against the exorbitant charges of the corner grocery and meat shops. In March of 1916 the Interborough Rapid Transit Company of New York started a chain of co-operative stores to lower the cost of living to its employees. After less than two years' experience it was compelled to acknowledge the failure of the scheme. The employees could not be induced to patronize them in sufficient numbers to make the co-operative effort pay.

The joint action of man is far less intelligent than his individual action. Man is not yet sufficiently socialized to co-operate on a large scale, except perhaps in time of war. The failure of our attempts at such co-operation is proof that we need education for co-operation. We have not yet learned to exercise collective intelligence and to assert collective power. Before the ideal of social co-operation can be fully realized, it will be necessary to establish instrumentalities of co-operation, commissions and bureaus which shall perform for us certain collective industrial functions just as our political representatives are now performing certain collective political functions. Among such instrumentalities would be public employment bureaus, vocational and educational advisory boards, bureaus regulating occupations, wages, prices, profits, and conditions of manufacture and employment. Occasional investigations will not solve the problem. Co-operation requires the establishment of permanent instrumentalities for the prevention of competitive waste.

The forms of democracy are useless unless each generation is trained in the methods of their use. We have been zealous to hand down to each generation the technique of freedom and the checks on arbitrary government: the right to assemble, the right to keep and bear arms, the right to be secure from seizure, the right of trial by jury, the right of free speech and of a free press. (See Ross: *Social Control*.) Similarly, in order to make the instrumentalities of co-operation effective, we must train each generation in the use of these instrumentalities, in the custom of meeting together for the interchange of ideas of common interest, in the means of checking private selfishness, in the spirit of self-denial, and in zeal for the common good.

Social Initiative

The ideal of social initiative can be most easily developed within a homogeneous group which has acquired a degree of group consciousness and a spirit of co-operation. Initiative, whether individual or social, is the expression of a need. It is an expression of resistance to unsatisfactory conditions, and not a mere passive mastery of a task. It demands independence of thought, self-reliance, and critical thinking. When it is manifested in a group, it is something more than the sum total of the initiative of its individual members. A group of boys working together will think of things, will do things that no individual boy working alone would ever think of doing, and the sum total of their collective performance is much greater than the total if each boy were working alone. Group initiative is rare in primitive groups except during times of social stress. It requires a high degree of co-ordination among its individual members. Only in highly developed democratic groups does social initiative become the mode of action.

Thorndike says: "The active virtues of citizenship are self-reliance, initiative and originality." Unfortunately these virtues are not always encouraged by the teachers in our schools.

The pupils who are best liked by the teachers and therefore most encouraged, are frequently those who are most docile, passive, and obedient. The boy with initiative is too often considered a bad boy. This is also true of a group which manifests social initiative. Such initiative is usually looked upon as incipient rebellion, and every autocratic means is used for its suppression. In defense of the teachers it may be said that these sporadic manifestations of instinctive group initiative in the schoolroom are not usually directed toward very high ends. The objective of the group may be nothing more than a day's vacation, or a school picnic, or a day for wearing some outlandish garb or decoration; but however silly this manifestation may be to an adult, the germ of social initiative should be recognized and the tendency toward concerted action, self directed by the group, should be encouraged rather than repressed.

In the ideal democracy toward which we are striving, group initiative will be one of the realized ideals. Each individual will adapt his work and his play to the good of the group; he will do his best to direct the activity of the group toward useful ends; he will improve himself and will encourage the improvement of others; he will search for new tasks and new accomplishments; he will be sufficiently interested in the work of others to make helpful suggestions and to render actual assistance. The group as a whole will make and enforce its own laws, not for the benefit of any particular locality or selfish interest, but for the good of all; the whole group will recognize a common interest and make common endeavor to promote the progress and insure the happiness of all its members.

Social Justice

When Plato was seeking a definition of the term justice he found it necessary to construct an ideal republic in which each person and each class of society worked harmoniously with all the others. The harmony of relationship in which no one imposed upon another; in which each gave the best that was within him and in turn received from all their best, was what he conceived to be the highest form of justice.

The forces which control a democracy are moral. One of the most fundamental of these forces is the sense of justice. It is found at every level and in every quarter of society. Whether it is innate or whether it is a social product, it is "the only power that can settle things so that they will stay settled." There is perhaps no other virtue in the government of society which will more closely join the individuals into one harmonious body than the administration of justice; and there is perhaps no other weakness in the government of society which will more effectively sharpen class consciousness, whet class hatred and tend to loosen all the social bonds than injustice. Justice means fair play in the game. Our present social organization gives each man a chance to play. If some of the players, because of their superior strength or ability, take unfair advantage of the others, and society does not assert its collective strength in the enforcement of the rules of the game, "the time may come when the opponents of individual initiative and of private capital will point to injustice as the necessary result of our present system, and will make every effort to destroy it." (Ross: *Sin and Society*.)

Some of the first lessons in social justice may be learned in the plays of childhood. Clean sportsmanship will at least suggest, if it will not insure, clean business and clean politics. Clean sportsmanship requires that the competitors shall not cheat, not play "for keeps" or money; that they abide by the decisions of the umpire; that they permit their opponents to present their side of the argument; that they refuse special favors or privileges; that they play the game according to the rules; that they show uniform courtesy, even to their opponents; that they protest against taking advantage of an opponent when he is down; that they protest against taking advantage of cripples or other unfortunates; that they defend those who are unjustly attacked; that they claim no more than their full share; that they accept defeat gracefully; that they accept victory graciously; that they give each other a square deal in the distribution of materials, tools, rewards, honors, and opportunities.

The social ideal of justice for the larger society will include equality of opportunity for every citizen in the land; fair play in business and in politics; a square deal for even the humblest worker; the proper respect for the rights of the minority; the proper respect for the integrity of every individual personality; and the placing of reasonable limits upon our present *laissez-faire* doctrine. The realization of the ideal of social justice will mean the establishment of the Golden Rule in all human affairs and relationships.

Social Control

Every well-organized society devises means for the control of its own members. In primitive groups, the control may be entirely autocratic, with the strongest man acting as chief, having vested in him the power of life and death and the full destiny of the tribe. In more progressive and intelligent groups, social control tends to be vested more and more in the individual members. If every individual in society were socially motivated and supplied with a perfect intelligence, government would be entirely unnecessary. It requires no argument to show that we are still far from such a goal. However, a reasonable ideal of social control, and therefore a worthwhile objective of social education, is the regulation of human conduct with a minimum utilization of the machinery of government.

Social control must begin with the self-control of each individual citizen. This truth is admirably expressed in the second law, The Law of Self-Control, in the *The Children's Code of Morals*, published by the National Institution for Moral Instruction, as follows:

> The good American controls himself. Those who best control themselves can best serve their country.
> 1. I will control my *tongue*, and will not allow it to speak mean, vulgar, or profane words.
> 2. I will control my *temper* and will not get angry when people or things displease me.
> 3. I will control my *thoughts*, and will not allow a foolish wish to spoil a wise purpose.

The law of self-control for each individual will also mean the inhibition of debasing practices, the formation of the habit of cheerfulness, or making one's self agreeable, and of trying to be pleasant in difficult situations. The person who truly controls himself will not be sulky or quarrelsome; will keep his mind free from worry; will be willing to confess his own mistakes and to make reparation if within his power. He will learn to persevere in spite of failure; will do his best even when a task is disagreeable and praise is not always forthcoming; will make the best of his misfortunes and take his disappointments bravely.

In a closely knit group where there is a spirit of social loyalty and a sense of social responsibility, social control is easily established. Once a certain standard is accepted by all the members of a group, this standard becomes a tradition, and tends to exercise control over each of its members. Every new member joining the group unconsciously absorbs the ideals or standards of the group. "This is one of our traditions" probably has more force in influencing the conduct of each member of a group than any written law could ever have. Whoever fails to conform to these unwritten standards is frowned upon by all the other members.

The ideal of social control will include obedience to law, obedience to proper authority, the suppression of exaggerated individualism, the willingness to let the law take its course rather than to resort to mob violence, and self-control in word and action. It will also include the training of the whole community in the art of self-direction, and in the use of social force to punish those whose offenses are not so much against individuals as against the entire social body: exploiters of the weak, traitors to private faith, betrayers of public trust, "men who steal elections, who make merchandise of the law, who make justice a mockery, who pervert good customs, who foil the plan of public intent, who pollute the wells of knowledge, who dim the ideals of youth." (Ross: *Sin and Society*.) To bring these modern enemies of society to task and to hold them under control, organized society will need to acquire the use of the weapon of public opinion. The acquisition of the use of this weapon, no less than the ability to detect the fine-spun crimes of modern times, will be among the difficult tasks of social education, if the ideal of social control be accepted as one of its important objectives.

Tolerance

If the ideal of social sympathy is fully inculcated, the ideal of toleration will not need to be made explicit. A full measure of sympathy and the attitude of trying to get one's neighbor's viewpoint will tend to produce an attitude of tolerance. An attitude of tolerance means respect for the convictions of others in matters of custom and religion. Even in America, where the ideal of religious freedom has been taught for many decades, it is still far from realization. The ideal of tolerance will include not only religious freedom, but also freedom of opinion and speech in other matters of general interest, appreciation of the good in others, open-mindedness, and a recognition of the reasons for the difference in the viewpoints of others.

Reverence

The Ordinance of 1787 contains this paragraph: "Religion, morality, and knowledge being necessary for good government and the happiness of mankind, schools and the means of education shall forever be encouraged."

Reverence is a religious ideal. It includes, first of all, a reverent attitude toward God, the church and the sacred scriptures. It implies respectful behavior toward the representatives of the church, and especially when in a place of worship. It means the maintenance of a respectful demeanor during the performance of religious ceremonies, and a feeling of veneration toward such objects and ideas as are considered sacred by others.

It will not be necessary to urge the ideal of reverence to the extent that it has been done in China. A reasonable emphasis, however, seems necessary at the present, if for no other reason than to checkmate the rather widespread attitude of making light of sacred things. The attitude of reverence should make an individual a better citizen. All stable civilizations have emphasized reverence as a desirable quality in a citizen. "The life history of a culture or civilization is frequently the history of a religion, . . . the religious element affording a sanction for the moral and social beliefs."

The attitude of respect for things religious may tend to carry over to venerable persons and institutions. The respectful and reverential man will venerate tradition and law. He will be respectful toward the expert. He will show respect toward the aged. In some foreign countries it is the custom to celebrate the birthdays of the grandparents. In America it is more often the custom to celebrate the birthdays of the children. It may be that the spirit of liberty in our country, the striving for equality, have tended to weaken our response toward the things that we would naturally venerate. If this is true, social education will need to set up new standards, and use such methods as will restore in our American people the ideal and the attitude of reverence.

Faith

While the ideal of faith is a religious ideal primarily, it is inconceivable that a democracy can be developed to perfection if this ideal be absent. A former generation believed that the problems of democracy could be solved by means of science, but it has been found that science will not solve them all, for democracy is itself an unrealized ideal. It is an ideal which could hardly have arisen in a scientific age. "Democracy, whose very essence is idealism, should become frankly and avowedly religious. . . . A religion that is to promote and sustain democracy must first of all be a religion of faith in man . . . [that] far transcends anything imagined hitherto . . . For democracy demands that we shall believe not in great and good men merely, and not merely in the ordinary run of people, but in all the people; that we shall have the confidence that they are able or will become able to govern themselves and to form a society where equal rights and opportunities and even-handed justice shall everywhere obtain. It is the biggest faith history has to show. If it be not a religious faith, there never was such a thing; and if it do not need all the religion a man can muster, religion never was needed for anything." (McGiffert, in *Religious Education*, Vol. XIV, pp. 157-158.)

CHAPTER III

THE PROBLEM OF METHODS

If the objectives which have been proposed be accepted provisionally, the next problem will be to determine how ideals and attitudes can be taught.

This problem naturally falls into three subdivisions: what must be the content of the curriculum, what methods must be employed, and what administrative agencies must be utilized to make our program of social education most effective. These problems are so closely related and their solutions are so interdependent, that they may be considered together. None of them can be solved without careful experimentation, and it may be a long time before all of them are completely solved. The best that can be done now is to adhere to such principles as have been found serviceable, and to give careful trial to new proposals before they are accepted.

The difficulty of this problem becomes apparent when it is realized that the ordinary processes of learning which are utilized in the formation of specific bonds, as in habits and knowledge, will need to be supplemented, or at least will need a new emphasis, if it is purposed to join a series of situations with a generalized response. A further difficulty is found in the fact that the psychology of the emotions which are manifested when men act collectively, is still very little understood. It will be assumed throughout this discussion that perhaps the best part of social education is conveyed by means of the emotions. Faith in this assumption and in the possibilities of education are eloquently expressed by Benjamin Kidd, in his *Science of Power*, in which he stoutly maintains that social heredity, the environment of ideals and traditions, is incomparably more important for civilization than the biological heredity stressed by the scientist, for the very reason that "through the emotion of the ideal, and through this course alone, the collective will can be concentrated and directed over long periods of time to particular ends." To quote further:

"If but one-half of the intelligence and effort [devoted to war] were directed to [education] . . . the outlook of humanity on nearly every fundamental matter [could] be changed in a single generation (p. 106) . . . . If the incoming generation of men were submitted to a new collective inheritance, including in particular its psychic elements, . . . a great [improvement would take place] in the world, appearing to the observer as if a fundamental alteration in human nature had suddenly taken place on a universal scale (p. 114). The immense potentiality of this collective heredity is due to two things . . . in the first place to [an] accumulation of recorded knowledge, . . . in the second place, and far more distinctly, to the creation and transmission of the collective heredity, of that psychic element which consists of ideas and idealisms that rest on emotion, and which are conveyed to the young under the influence of psychic emotion (p. 115). The laws of social emotion . . . have a different physical basis in the human organism from the laws of mind, which express themselves in reason. There is no ideal . . . dreamed of by any dreamer which cannot be realized within the lifetime of those around him (p. 120). The idealisms of mind and spirit conveyed to the young . . . under the influence of the social passion are absolutely limitless in their effects. . . But it has never been seen actually in being, directed and controlled by civilization (p. 122). The mind of the West . . . has failed to understand the emotion of the ideal. It has not grasped either the nature, or the magnitude, of the management of its function in the future of civilization (p. 171).

"The existing individuals must be rendered capable of subordinating their minds, their lives, and all the interests within the span of their lives, to an ideal which is beyond their lives, and which may even at times be beyond their understanding (p. 225).

"The West knows practically nothing of the science of emotion . . . in its most important manifestations which are in the social integration. Every Western writer on the subject, with the prominent exception of Mr. William McDougall, . . . thinks and theorizes about the facts of emotion almost as if emotion related only to the individual . . . . The science of emotion in its collective aspects . . . is practically a sealed book" (p. 193).

Nevertheless, for countless ages the emotions of men have been successfully played upon by ecclesiastical, civil and military leaders. Great institutions have been established and held together for long periods of time by the cohesive power of these emotions. The methods and devices that have proved successful in the manipulation of these integrative forces are not yet scientifically understood, although some of them doubtless have a sound empirical basis. It still remains for scientific experimentation to reveal the underlying principles and to determine what are the *best* methods of procedure. In the meantime, educational practice will necessarily be guided by the assumptions which are either expressed or implied in the generally accepted educational theories of the present time. The most generally accepted of these assumptions may be summed up and stated as follows:

1. *Social education can best be given in a social environment.* Dewey says, "You cannot teach a child to swim unless you take him to the water." The gang, clique, or neighborhood group is the natural gymnasium in which the qualities of citizenship must be exercised. These virtues can best be evoked and strengthened in the environment of the group. The more closely knit the group organization, the more powerfully will the group standards be impressed upon each individual. Lee says, in *Play in Education:* "The lack of definite social pressure is the weakest point in our present civilization. We need for our salvation the compelling influence of a particular group, with definite standards and stern transmission of them. With the primitive but definite ideals of barbarian society something very precious has been lost. We need in some form that compactness of social structure, capable of receiving and transmitting definite standards of behavior, without subjection to which the future citizen is denied the most important element in education."

In the absence of tribal organization, our modern educational system must approximate its conditions by the creation of artificially organized groups which shall be as closely knit as possible. Sometimes a school can be so organized. Sometimes it will be necessary to form extra-school organizations, which will appeal to the gregarious instincts of developing boys and girls, and which will provide group activities that seem to each individual worth while.

The Boy Scouts and similar organizations are adapted to perform this function. They furnish the motive for joining a group, if a motive be wanting, and they provide conditions under which the group tends to become closely knit in fellowship,—community of interests and close personal contacts. It is under these conditions that the interplay of minds becomes intense and the standards of conduct which are accepted within the group through the compelling power of social approval and disapproval, are impressed upon each individual member of the organization.

2. The second assumption is that *standards should be built up within the group and not imposed from without.* Only the recognized leaders of a group are able to modify its standards. A teacher or a policeman may hold a group in subjection by the sheer strength of his personality or authority, but until he is accepted by the group as an "insider," his influence will not extend beyond his authority. It is impossible for an outsider to break the will of a gang. His efforts are likely to have the opposite effect. Any individual member of the group who in a moment of weakness is induced to "tell tales" on the others, not only loses caste with the organization, but through his very treason strengthens the other members in their determination to adhere to the accepted standards.

Whoever would acquire the art of modifying the standards of a group must become a member of the group and must build the standards from within. Here also the Boy Scouts are rendering a valuable service to the cause of social education. The leaders of the group, if they are qualified to do their work, become accepted members. They gain the affection and the respect of all the individual members. They share in the labors and in the pleasures of the organization, and learn to adjust themselves to the moods and caprices of the group mind. They are able to hold themselves in the background so that the natural leadership and initiative of the group may assert itself on every possible occasion; and they are able to assume the leadership themselves when the situation demands the guidance of adult wisdom and experience.

3. The third assumption is that *every modification of the standards of the group and every moral readjustment in the minds of the individuals composing the group can best be brought about by means of grappling with vital issues.* These issues must be related to the personal experiences or at least to the interesting vicarious experiences of the individual members. The most vital issues are those which tend to grow out of their immediate group life. Dr. Frank M. McMurry says that a series of issues which are vital to the student constitutes a curriculum. Dr. Dewey says that "ideas must be acquired in a vital way in order to become moving ideas, motive forces in the guidance of conduct." The vitalizing element is emotional. It arises from the needs or interests of the individual in relation to his group life. When a situation presents itself which demands a response on the part of all the individual members of the group, it becomes a vital issue. There will be interplay of minds. Facts will be brought out and information sought in the adjustment of the issue. It is evident that under these circumstances the information or knowledge that is acquired will find its proper place; namely, in the service of purpose. Professor F. W. Foerster says (*Jugendlehre*, p. 7): "It is not what we know, but for what purpose we know it that is of importance in genuine education. It is not the fact that we can read and write that really matters, but what we read and write."

Taking advantage of the vital issues that incidentally grow out of group relationships, and creating such issues if they do not present themselves spontaneously, is nothing more nor less than the project method applied to social education. The content of the curriculum, as well as its logical or other arrangement, will be quite dependent upon the issues that grow out of the social relationships. To set up a standard when no social need is felt, to provide information when there is no interest, to attempt to produce a moral response when there is no situation to evoke it, may be worse than useless; certainly such procedure is often not only barren of the desired results, but deadening to the sensibilities of the individual when at a later time the proper situation is produced.

Here again scouting renders a valuable service to the cause of social education. As Dean Russell expresses it: "The curriculum of scouting is not its most striking feature. It is the method. As a systematic scheme of leading boys to do the right thing and to inculcate right habits it is almost ideal. Habits are fixed and opportunities are afforded for initiative, self-control, self-reliance, self-direction. These are implicit in all educational effort." The Scout program is valuable because it creates the setting, the general situation out of which many vital issues grow. The activities of the group are of importance to each member. Moral battles are fought and victories won in the settlement of disputes, in the determination of types of activity to be pursued, and in the actual performance of tasks which the group has set for accomplishment.

4. The fourth assumption is that *the positive social virtues can best be strengthened by means of actual participation.* The activities of the group must be co-operative: The boys must play together and work together; they must participate not only in the activities of the small group in which they hold their immediate membership, but also in many of the activities of the larger community of which they are a part. During the war our wisest teachers utilized their golden opportunity to teach citizenship by means of participation projects: Visiting the sick, war gardening, selling Liberty Bonds, investing in Savings Stamps, and working for the Red Cross. Such participation is useful not only because it tends to fix certain habits of participation, but also because it tends to establish certain ideals and attitudes. The development of a social conscience, of a community of interests, the bringing to bear of social pressures, will require a technique which is difficult to create unless there is social participation. By helping to make the rules of the game, the individual will learn from experience how agreements are reached by compromise, and thus come to realize the advantages of co-operative activity. By being subjected to social pressure he learns to respond to it. By taking part in the projects of the group he will learn that he is expected to do his share of the work. By exercising his conscience on the live moral issues he becomes sensitive to the principles involved. We have long utilized and developed a certain amount of social responsibility on the lighter side of life. It is necessary for us to carry this method further and induce the sense of responsibility and the ability to act

collectively by requiring group action when the more important social relationships of the boy are involved.

It is hardly necessary to say that the teacher or leader of the group must learn how to sink his own authority. Nothing will stifle group initiative sooner than to have a strong man or woman assume responsibility for its direction. The Scout movement has been fortunate in that many of its leaders are able, temporarily, to forget their own authority in order that the group might exercise initiative in carrying out its own activities. To be sure, these group activities must be curbed by the leader if there is any strong tendency for the group to stray too far from the purpose for which it was organized.

5. The fifth assumption is *the validity of group motivation.* Thorndike says, "Motivation must be strong enough so that the individual will act and act again and be dissatisfied by other types of action." In a group of Boy Scouts the leader constantly aims at social motivation. This is done by praising the group as a whole rather than any individual member of it; by setting up group objectives to be accomplished rather than individual objectives. A game of ball with a neighboring troop, a hike in the woods with the rest of them, a swim together in the gymnasium, a week-end out at the seashore,—these objectives are for the entire group, and the individual is made to feel that he is to contribute his share toward the success of the group enterprise; as much as possible individual feelings are left out of account.

Dewey says: "Mere learning is individualistic. The methods of instruction, their general spirit, must emphasize construction and giving out. Each one must be taught to give something. This shifts the center of gravity from absorption which is selfish to a service which is social." Social motivation grows in an atmosphere of social service, where each one is taught by means of active participation in group affairs to give something, to do something for the welfare of the group. Long-continued participation under such conditions will result in an "habituation to a sound moral working order." Social education must furnish the motive for all other forms of education,—vocational, physical and cultural; otherwise the *purpose* of the efforts will vitiate their results. Even the search for culture, if it is prompted by selfish motive, may be a vice rather than a virtue. Social education must set the goal, not of material achievement or individual success, but of the service of mankind. It must create the desire in every individual for a social solidarity, and take the ideal of service as its chief end.

6. The sixth assumption is that *the virtues of the small group should be strengthened and used as a basis for the strengthening of the virtues that will be useful in the larger group.* Each individual must learn to adjust himself to group life. The first adjustments that he learns to make are naturally those in the family circle and in the immediate neighborhood. The later and perhaps more impersonal adjustments to the larger community are interpreted in the light of his earlier and more personal adjustments. In the family and neighborhood group he must learn not to be quarrelsome, he must not tell lies, he must not commit injury against any member of the group, he must not be unjust, he must not steal, he must not be untruthful. In fact, he must deport himself toward the members of the small group in such a way that his presence will be entirely acceptable to all concerned. It is a mistake for a teacher or leader to combat the small group virtues because they sometimes seem to be detrimental to the life of the larger group: the large group virtues naturally grow out of the small group virtues, by an extension of sympathy and social consciousness. Gradually the small group must be made conscious of its dependence upon larger units. This extension of consciousness must be supplemented by expansion and extension of the duties that are to be performed. Education for citizenship at this point demands definite information of the duties and responsibilities which the members of the small group owe to the larger unit to which they belong. Such information can be supplied in the course of the regular schoolroom activities and it will be welcomed by the learners if it is supplied in response to a conscious need. The conscious need must arise from the adjustments which the learner is making in his everyday relationships to the larger social unit of which he finds himself a member.

It is here again that scouting performs a valuable service in the training of young patriots by making them conscious of these larger relationships. Dean Russell says, "Under the leadership of patriotic teachers there are aroused ambitions and feelings that make for patriotism, impulses to do good and be good from the national standpoint." The Boy Scouts in almost every community are brought by wise leadership into these larger relationships; they render service on the street corner, assisting the police, acting as guides, messengers, agents of law and order. This contact with city, state and national life gives the small group a feeling of importance, a feeling of significance, and brings it into vital relationship with the larger group. Under such circumstances it is not difficult to foresee that a troop of Boy Scouts tends rapidly to become a group of splendid patriotic young citizens. The order of development or of extension of group consciousness would naturally be from the small to the next larger unit in size, from the gang or troop to the school, from the school to the neighborhood, from the neighborhood to the town, from the town to the county, from the county to the state, from the state to the nation, from the nation to the world.

7. The seventh assumption is that *the limits and the conflicts between the small and the large group relationships must be clearly defined and situations must be provided for solving problems in which such conflicts occur.* Small group loyalties are a menace to society at large, unless upon these loyalties there are grafted motives for the welfare of the larger group. "The dispositions to revolve, act, and serve solely within the social orbits of local component and constituent groups is probably still produced and justified in large measure by the traditions and vestigial customs surviving into modern democracies from ages of autocratic control from without." (Dr. Snedden.) One of the first steps in directing these provincial or small group loyalties, which, when undirected, have an anti-social bearing, is to throw the small group into contact with other groups. Such contact will give a perspective and lay the foundation of the concept of a larger group life. Each small group should establish relationship with other small groups, and all should be made conscious of their dependence upon each other and especially of their dependence on a larger unit. These relationships may be established by means of inter-group plays and games, or other forms of inter-group activity.

It must not be assumed that the habits which have been acquired in the small group will necessarily transfer to the inter-group and large group relationships. When the situation is entirely new, old habits will need to be readjusted or new habits will need to be formed. The knowledge which was acquired in the small group life will probably transfer to the large group relationships; it needs only to be extended as the individual progresses into larger and ever larger group relationships. Whether the ideals and attitudes that are acquired in the small group extend their functions to the larger relationships is still a problem to be solved.

8. The eighth assumption is that *the personality of the teacher* or leader is a fundamental factor in the establishment of standards and traditions. "As is the teacher so is the school." The concrete reality of a living personality in daily contact with the child is perhaps the most effective source of his ideals. There is nothing more contagious than personal example. The virtues and the vices of the leader tend to be imitated by the members of the group. The attitudes, tastes, prejudices, and ideals of the leader tend to be unconsciously absorbed. The sum total of the leader's attitudes, tastes, prejudices and ideals constitute his personality. Ideals thus become "inspiring" when they are exemplified in the life of an individual, and the influence of such an individual leader is limited only by the positive or negative emotional reactions on the part of those who are being led.

"American children decidedly surpass German children in the range and variety of their ideals . . . . Meumann believes that [this] points to fundamental differences in school instruction. German pedagogy lays too great stress on mere intellectual acquisition, too little on the cultivation of personality. If this be granted, it follows that it is highly important to give systematic and definite attention in the school to the inculcation of ideals." (Monroe: *Principles of Secondary Education,* p. 290.)

9. The ninth assumption is *the utility of mottoes, slogans, shibboleths, taboos, and other words or phrases in unifying or organizing for each individual the standards which he is accepting from the group.* Examples of such mottoes stated in the negative are: "Don't be a quitter." "Don't be yellow." "Don't be a mucker," "a squealer," "a pussy-footer." "Don't be a cad." Other examples stated positively are: "Be square," "Be honest."

"The 'fair play' boys," "The square dealers." The advantage of using a slogan is to force the individual who has subscribed to the standards of the group to fall into line immediately when the slogan is uttered.

It is not only boys but grown people who have discovered the value of the slogan and of the taboo. Arguments are often silenced by such words as "anarchist," "traitor," "socialist," and other taboos which have been accepted by society as means of social defense. The wise leader or teacher makes use of such mottoes to tie together a number of good motives and ideals. By creating this motto consciousness, he sets up a constant reminder in the individual that he is to be loyal to the group standard. It is possible for such standards to be wrongly chosen. A group of boys in a slum neighborhood called themselves "the toughs." They would not join the Boy Scouts because they considered them too refined; they tried to live up to their standard of being "tough" and probably succeeded quite well.

In the moral conduct of the adult it is very often true that a word or a phrase proves to be a man's salvation or his downfall. Professor James pointed this out years ago. Once a sin is labeled as such, people will shrink from it; it is a question of labeling it; the label must be ready at hand if the process of labeling is to be performed automatically and promptly when the occasion arises.

10. The tenth assumption is *in the validity of the law of effect*. The best way to build an inhibitive habit in any individual against an anti-social practice, is to associate the practice with dissatisfaction or annoyance. One such annoyance may be enough to form a permanent inhibition. The burnt child dreads the fire. The burning was an annoyance. The boy who is caught in the act of stealing or cheating and who finds social pressure and disapproval against such practice, may be permanently cured the moment he feels the sense of shame. In a former generation the clergyman tried to arouse his hearers to a "consciousness of sin." This is good educational psychology. A strong feeling of dissatisfaction will set up inhibitive tendencies that will stand in the way of a reaction when the next temptation comes.

The counterpart of the law of annoyance is the law of satisfaction. Dewey says that "inhibition is not sufficient; instincts and impulses must be concentrated upon positive ends." When a boy has done a good deed, when he has rendered a social service, when he has shown himself trustworthy, his right action should be accompanied by satisfaction. This satisfaction may be the result of an inner "squaring" of his action with his accepted standards. Or it may be the result of the approval of his superiors and of his equals of his right action. Too much cannot be made of this. Right action should be accompanied by feelings of satisfaction. If an individual has stood up against a crowd in doing what he thought to be right, he should be commended for his courage by those whose approval he craves. The consequences of his right action should also bring him a feeling of permanent satisfaction. Only thus can the tendency to do right be strengthened and made permanent.

11. The eleventh assumption is that *ideals and attitudes are generalizations of specific habits.* "Build from specific habits by the inductive method," says Snedden. "Prejudices and attitudes may grow out of specific habits," says Bagley, "as when the habits of Sunday observance, established in early childhood, become more or less explicitly formulated as ideals and gradually come to express themselves as prejudices which make the lack of observance a matter of discomfort and annoyance. . . . From the specific habit of accuracy developed by mathematics, one comes gradually to idealize accuracy as a method of procedure that will bring desirable results in other fields." (*Educational Values*, pp. 45 ff.) It is natural for the mind to go from the concrete to the abstract. The boy who is taught to tip his hat to his mother or to his teacher does not need to be told to generalize. As soon as he has formed the specific habit, he generalizes it; and henceforth he tips his hat to every lady. "Tastes are built up on the foundation of individual experiences," says Judd. Genetically, our ideals emerge when our emotionalized experiences are generalized, that is, when they are raised to the level of an idea.

12. The final assumption is that *ideals are best strengthened through emotional experiences.* This is almost a corollary of the law of effect. No amount of reasoning can move a man to act unless his feelings are also involved. These feelings may not

be violent, they may not be outwardly manifest, but they are ever present as satisfiers and annoyers, influencing the selective activities of the mind. It is therefore easy to believe that our ideals are influenced by means of literature and music and other forms of art which appeal to the emotions. Our actions are determined by our loves and hates. The more powerful these emotions, the more effective are the ideals to which they are attached.

The cumulative effect of emotions when they are interacting in a crowd is still but little understood. It is a well known fact, however, that emotional effects are greatly heightened in the presence of a multitude. Religious fervor is intensified, a war spirit is spread, when men are congregated in meetings. It is for this reason that an English author, Mr. F. H. Hayward, in his *Spiritual Foundations of the Future* suggests the wider use of celebrations, pageants, ceremonials, dramatic representations, and other public performances as a means of stimulating emotional fervor in an assembled multitude and joining this fervor with such ideas of patriotism, religion, and human brotherhood as seem most desirable to be perpetuated.

CHAPTER IV

THE PROBLEM OF THE FUNCTION OF IDEALS AND ATTITUDES

One of the important problems to be solved before a broad program of social education can be built, is the problem of the function of ideals and attitudes. It is the purpose of this chapter, first, to set up the hypothesis that ideals and attitudes are among the resultants of education and that their function is to guide, control, and stabilize human conduct; and, second, to point out that this hypothesis is in agreement with the opinion of the majority of the world's educators, with the known laws of nature, and with the laws of learning in so far as they are understood.

The terms ideal and attitude will be used throughout this discussion in their generalized rather than in their specific sense. The function of specific ideals and attitudes is so generally admitted that it is hardly necessary to mention them. A boy who through experience forms the ideal of an erect carriage, or who acquires the attitude of respect to old age, will be quite likely to make the proper responses in every situation which is associated with his ideal or his attitude, for the reason that his specific ideal and attitude tend immediately to become habitual. The more highly generalized ideals and attitudes, however, are probably not so definitely linked up with habits.

It is known that there are great individual differences in the ability to generalize. A certain tribe in Africa is said to have a word for cat and a word for dog, but no word for animal. It is easy to believe that there are certain ideals so abstract, so highly generalized, that they would have no meaning, and certainly no compelling power, in the minds of individuals who are only slightly capable of abstract thought. It is equally easy to believe that a child which is capable of high intellectual and moral development may be led in successive steps from comprehension of, and obedience to, the ideal of clean hands to ever larger ideals—clean body, clean surroundings, cleanliness, health and holiness (using the latter word in its original and undistorted sense).

Ideals and attitudes will be used in this discussion in contradiction with all other resultants of education. Most theorizers on education would agree that the resultants of education in any individual may be roughly classified as knowledge and ideas, habits and skills, ideals and attitudes. Other terms which are sometimes employed, such as tastes, sentiments, beliefs, appreciations and prejudices, may readily be subsumed under the three general rubrics which will be used in the discussion throughout this chapter.

The function of knowledge in social education is so generally agreed upon that it is hardly necessary to mention it in passing. "Knowledge is an instrument, not an end," says Bagley. It affects conduct by bringing "consciously to bear upon the problems of adjustment the related factors of past experience. It may be used to direct conduct to unworthy ends as readily as to worthy ends." The function of knowledge is to guide in the realization of purpose. Without such purpose it has no function to perform. Dean Russell says: "Mere knowledge does not guarantee citizenship." Miss Bronner says: "Ideas about morality do not transform themselves automatically into good character or conduct." Swift says, "There seems to be an impression that if we give a child information enough he will in some time and in some way apply it to the problems of life, but the facts do not justify this view." (*Mind in the Making*, pp. 70-87 and 324.) The ideo-motor theory has been discredited. (See Thorndike, *Educational Psychology*, Vol. I, pp. 177 ff.) It is no longer assumed that knowledge of right is a guarantee of right doing. "Until educators learn to think of the final purpose of education in other terms than mastery of so much knowledge . . . progress will necessarily be slow," says Monroe. (*Principles of Secondary Education*, p. 762.)

Nevertheless, it must not be assumed, because knowledge is secondary in its socializing value, that instruction in knowledge is therefore to be neglected. On the contrary, social education will foster the dissemination of knowledge. "What we can well call the *problems* confronting the citizen—questions and issues of economic, political, ethical, municipal, national, international, financial, and sociological nature—are increasingly of a kind that can not be resolved by well intentioned compliance and kindly initiative alone." (David Snedden, in *The International Journal of Ethics*, Vol. XXX, No. 1.) "Knowledge may furnish a basis for mutual sympathy and understanding necessary to adequate social solidarity;" and it is necessary in the solution of the problems of modern civilization.

The social function of habits and skills is not quite so clear and will require brief definition and explanation. The word habit will be used here in the narrow sense "to mean a relatively simple acquired tendency to act, usually described in terms of outward conduct." A skill may be defined as a "complex of simple habits, used with greater consciousness of the end in view. Considered in themselves, habits and skills are only mechanisms or tools of conduct, and are not to be considered either as moral or immoral." "A habit is the easy channel which frees personality for fuller and wider action. As a man attains higher levels, he performs higher and more complex tasks. His very habits often become out of date and a clog on progress unless they are adjusted to growing needs. So far as our conduct is shaped by habit, it is shaped passively."

The limited function of habits and skills is shown by the impossibility of training each individual for all the actions which he is to perform in later life. In certain narrow vocations every action may be anticipated. The factory worker, the clerk, is taught every movement as if he were part of a machine. In the larger relationships of life, however, situations are not always simple and ready made. New adjustments are frequently necessary. The man who learned to say "Yes ma'am" to his teacher is put to shame if he makes this stereotyped response to a polite gentleman. Our simple and early formed habits of obedience, when they persist, are often handicaps in the performance of our duties as full-fledged and responsible citizens.

It would indeed be possible to create an orderly world, a world of perfect "moral" behavior, if all human action were on the plane of habit; but it would be the kind of order which is found in a prison, "well-regulated" by the older standards, and the kind of "moral" behavior which is found in a marching army, where each individual is controlled by the commands of an officer. However, such conduct could not be called moral except by a stretch of the imagination, for it would not furnish even the illusion of choice; moreover, common sense tells us that every individual is often confronted by situations for which he has no acquired responses, where it is necessary for him to act without previous training. The adjustments which he makes to these new and unexpected situations may be assumed to depend partly upon the knowledge and ideas which he can summon out of his accumulated store of experience, and partly upon the ideals and attitudes which dominate the purposes of his life, or which determine the way in which situations are interpreted.

If it were true that all human conduct is on the plane of habit, it would be necessary to provide a specific habit for every specific situation in which the future citizen would find himself, or leave him helpless when he confronts a new situation. In order to teach a citizen to be thrifty, he would need to be trained to save pennies, nickels, dimes, quarters, fifty-cent pieces, dollars, and so on for every coin and denomination of the realm. Not only that: he would also need to be trained to save paper, pins, pencils, erasers, food, clothing, shoes and every other article of domestic and industrial value of which he would ever find himself the possessor.

There is a grain of truth in the contention that if the boy is trained to save dimes, he will be more likely to save dimes than other coins; in fact, a boy so trained will change the quarters and half dollars which he earns into dimes for the purpose of inserting the dimes into his bank. But this fact does not prove that it is impossible to teach a boy to be thrifty. If it were impossible to teach a boy to be thrifty the educational process would be on the low level of animal training, with the performance of tricks as the great objective. The well-educated individual would be the one who had learned to respond automatically to the largest number of desirable tricks. Such a one would automatically save pennies, nickels, dimes, and all the other coins. He would automatically conserve his health, he would habitually make the best use of his time, he would not waste food, or clothing, because he would have acquired specific habits of response to the largest number of situations in which economy is possible.

What is said of thrift may be said of the large social objectives which we have provisionally set up. If man had nothing more than the capacity of forming specific habits of response, it would be futile to call a man loyal. We could only say that he had formed a habit of being loyal to his father or mother, or school group, or his gang. If there were only specific loyalties it would not be possible to train an individual to be loyal except by training him for each and every particular situation demanding loyalty in which we would wish him to respond in later life. The same may be said of what we have called responsibility. If man's reactions are all on the one plane of habit, there is no such thing as a "sense" of responsibility and the individual will need to be trained to be responsible in every situation in which he may later find himself placed.

These considerations lead to the main problem: What is the function of ideals and attitudes in social education? Is it possible by means of the methods herein proposed, or by other methods, to inculcate ideals and attitudes which shall be powerful enough to dominate human purposes? Is there foundation for the belief that ideals and attitudes may serve as general conduct-controls when specific responses are lacking? To what extent can education prepare the individual members of society to make ethical responses when confronted by situations which are entirely new and unforeseen? If it be granted, as Thorndike says, that "the one thing which education can do best is to establish those particular connections with ideas which we call knowledge, and those particular connections with acts which we call habits," is it also possible for education to establish connections with those general ideas which we call ideals and with those general habits which we call attitudes; and can it establish these connections in so vital a way that the ideals and attitudes will serve in the control of conduct? Unless it is possible to prove that such connections can be made and that they perform a vital function in directing the current of human lives, it will be useless to build broad programs for moral, religious and civic education. On the other hand, if it can be shown that there is a possibility of transfer of training from the school to the moral, civic and religious life of the outside world, the importance of inculcating proper ideals will be recognized, and broad programs of social education may confidently be undertaken.

Ideals and attitudes will be used in this discussion as used by a Committee on Education for Citizenship appointed by Dean James E. Russell from the faculty of Teachers College. "An ideal is probably best thought of as consisting of (I) a generalized notion or general concept used as a plan or standard of action, (II) the recognition and appreciation of the practical worth of this plan or standard, and (III) a tendency (habit) to accept and obey the plan or standard, to act it out in conduct. Unless these three elements are present, we cannot properly employ the term *ideal*." "An attitude is properly settled behavior, a settled manner of acting because of habitual feeling or opinion. Three factors or aspects are here present, (I) an habitual mode of thinking, (II) a settled interest; (III) a settled mode of acting as growing out of habitual feeling or thinking. These three aspects give rise to three types of attitudes, according as one or the other element is emphasized: (I) a "point of view" (apperceptive attitude); (II) an 'interest'; (III) an action attitude." "A point of view is frequently called an 'attitude of mind,' a 'mental set,' a 'mental background,' a 'perspective,' an 'appreciative basis.' In each of these terms, a settled mode of regarding or apperceiving a situation is clearly the predominant factor. In the case of an interest, as here used, there is equally clearly a settled disposition to pay attention to, to be interested in, or to learn more about the object of interest. For the action attitude there is unfortunately no adequate term in common use. . . . It includes almost equally the apperceptive and the action elements, both of which, however, have through extended practice become almost automatic in their action."

The ready assent which is hereby given to the definition of "ideal" as outlined above is not to be considered as a method of begging the question in the main problem. For it will still need to be shown that ideals as herein defined actually exist— in other words, that it is possible for a general concept to become attached to a feeling of worth and thereby given a tendency to express itself in conduct. This is also true of attitudes. If the definitions of "ideal" and "attitude" as given above be accepted, the problem of the function of ideals and attitudes is merely shifted to the problem of whether they exist at all.

Professor Woodworth, in his *Dynamic Psychology* (pp. 36 ff.), presents the two concepts of "mechanism" and "drive" which may be useful in the analysis of this problem. "One is the problem, how we do a thing, and the other is the problem of what induces us to do it." "The sensory nerve drives the motor center (which drives the muscle), being itself driven by a stimulus reaching the sense organ from without." Sometimes different nerve impulses come together, "with the result in some cases that one strengthens the other, and in some cases that one weakens or suppresses the other." The drive in some cases "is not entirely the local stimulus, but other centers in the brain and spinal cord, being themselves aroused from outside, furnish drive for the center that is directly responsible for the movement." "A nerve center, aroused to activity, does not in all cases relapse into quiescence, after a momentary discharge. Its state of activity may outlast the stimulus that aroused it, and this residual activity in one center may act as drive to another center; or, a center may be 'sub-excited' by an external stimulus that is not capable of arousing it to full discharge; and, while thus sub-excited, it may influence other centers, either by way of reinforcement or by way of inhibition." "The relationship between two mechanisms, such that one, being partially excited, becomes the drive of another, is especially significant in the case of what have been called 'preparatory and consummatory reactions' (by) Sherrington. A consummatory reaction is one of direct value to the animal—one directly bringing satisfaction—such as eating or escaping from danger." . . . "Preparatory reactions are only mediately of benefit to the organism, their value lying in the fact that they lead to, and make possible, a consummatory reaction." "That there is a persistent inner tendency towards the consummatory reaction is seen, when, for instance, a hunting dog loses the trail; . . . This seeking, not being evoked by any external stimulus (but rather by the absence of an external stimulus), must be driven by some internal force."

". . . The dog's behavior is to be interpreted as follows: the mechanism for a consummatory reaction, having been set into activity by a suitable stimulus, acts as a drive operating other mechanisms which give the preparatory reactions. Each preparatory reaction may be a response in part to some external stimulus, but it is facilitated by the drive towards the consummatory reaction. Not only are some reactions thus facilitated, but others . . . are inhibited. The dog on the trail does not stop to pass the time of day with another dog; he is too busy. . . ."

"Drive . . . is not essentially distinct from mechanism. The drive is a mechanism already aroused. . . . Any mechanism might be a drive. But it is the mechanisms directed towards consummatory reactions—whether of the simple sort seen in animals or of the more complex sort exemplified by human desires and motives—that are most likely to act as drives."

The natural drives are the instincts and native capacities, and especially those bodily and conscious states known as emotions, which closely accompany instinctive activities and the expression of native capacities. "The human mind has certain innate or inherited tendencies which are the essential springs or motive powers of all thought and action, whether individual or collective, and are the bases from which the character and will of individuals and of nations are gradually developed under the guidance of the intellectual faculties." (McDougall, *Social Psychology*, p. 19.)

But these native capacities and instinctive impulses are not the only motive powers of the human mind to thought and action, says the same author: "In the developed human mind there are springs of action of another class, namely, acquired habits of thought and action." (p. 42.)

It is with these acquired drives or motive powers that we are here chiefly concerned. How are they acquired? How does it come about that the earning of money, at first undertaken purely as a means to an end, gradually becomes the end itself? How does it come about that men acquire the "finest things in life . . . its generosities, its sacrifices, its renunciations, its achievements . . . (that) have but a restricted instinctive sanction?" (Colvin and Bagley, *Human Behavior*, pp. 150 ff.) How can the native drives of the human mind be manipulated, so that, like a ship sailing against the wind, an individual will struggle against the current of his most imperious natural desires?

"What a man is and does throughout life is a result of whatever constitution he has at the start and of all the forces that act upon it before and after birth. . . . The basis of intellect and character is (the) fund of unlearned tendencies. . . . They are the starting point for all education . . . . The aim of education is to perpetuate some of them, to eliminate some, and to modify or redirect others. They are perpetuated by providing the stimuli adequate to arouse them and give them exercise, and by associating satisfaction with their action. They are eliminated by withholding these stimuli so that they abort through disuse, or by associating discomfort with their action. They are redirected by substituting . . . another response instead of the undesirable original one, or by attaching the response to another situation in connection with which it works less or no harm, or even positive good." (Thorndike, *Educational Psychology*, Vol. I, pp. 2-4.)

The emotional element, rather than the cognitive and the conative elements, plays the leading role in the perpetuation, the elimination, and the redirection of the unlearned tendencies. The reason for this undoubtedly is that "emotion . . . represents or is correlative with the drive towards . . . consummatory reaction. . . . The emotions do not arise in the individual as the result of training. He learns to be afraid of certain objects, but he does not learn how to be afraid. All he needs in order to be afraid is to receive the proper stimulus, and then he is afraid by force of nature . . . . The stimuli that evoke these reactions change with experience, and their connections with the reactions are learned or acquired by the individual." (Woodworth, *Dynamic Psychology*, pp. 51-80.) In other words, the feelings, emotions, or driving forces in any individual are inborn and unchangeable. The direction which these driving forces take is entirely a matter of education. This truth is clearly expressed in Colvin and Bagley's *Human Behavior* (pp. 150 ff.):

"Moral culture consists primarily in shifting the emphasis which nature has placed upon certain acts and activities. We no longer need to fear the dark; the feelings of disgust and repulsion no longer need attach to certain objects that were dangerous in primitive life; but we *do* need to fear evil, and we *do* need to attach to certain tendencies that may have been very important in primitive life the feeling of disgust that will lead us to thrust them out of our presence. Aristotle, centuries ago, suggested that the primary problem of moral culture is to lead the individual to *love* the good and to *hate* the bad. Love and hate imply feelings and emotions that originally attach to certain instincts."

The first step in the solution of the problem of the function of ideals and attitudes, is to determine how the great emotional drives may be brought under control; how safety valves may be provided so that certain undesirable drives may "blow off steam" without setting in motion any of the preparatory and consummatory machinery; and how other drives may be detached from the objects which originally stimulate them to reaction, and become attached with their appropriate responses to other and often vastly different objects. There are at least five ways in which this may be done.

The first method is by the dissociation of a response from its natural stimulus. This may be accomplished by negative adaptation, as when uncongenial people learn to live together in peace; it may be accomplished by punishment or other disastrous experience, as when a burned child learns to dread the fire; and it may be accomplished by repeated failure in the pursuit of a certain aim. The unpleasant feelings associated with the performance of the act, tend to break the bonds between the stimulus and its original response.

A second method is by "the attachment of another response to an object and to the feelings that the object instinctively arouses. The combative instinct furnishes a good example. . . . If I ruthlessly take from a little child the object which he has appropriated and in which he finds pleasure, he will strike . . . and emit a cry of rage. . . . If my neighbor steals my horse . . . I must seek satisfaction, not with my fists . . . but through a due and proper process of law . . ." (Colvin and Bagley, *Human Behavior*, pp. 150 ff.) This change of behavior is accomplished by making the new response more satisfying than the primitive response. The old emotion of resentment is not repressed; it is attached to, and becomes the driving force for the new response.

A third way in which an unlearned tendency may be modified is by attaching an emotion with its characteristic response to a familiar situation which had never before evoked this emotion and response. This may be accomplished by associating satisfying emotions with desirable variations in conduct, as for example, when a boy is led by a wise teacher to accomplish successfully a task which he had hitherto hated, because he thought himself to be incompetent in this particular work. On the same principle a child may be led to admire the goldenrod, which he had hitherto despised, because his teacher whom he greatly loved, admired the goldenrod; or a wealthy old miser, who had never known the joy of giving, may suddenly discover what it means, when, touched by the whim of a moment, he amuses himself by making a gift to a ragged urchin.

A fourth method is by "the attachment of a natural reaction to a stimulus that is not its natural stimulus." (Woodworth, *Dynamic Psychology*, p. 81.) The Russian physiologist Pawlow performed an experiment by placing in a dog's mouth a substance which arouses a flow of saliva, and simultaneously ringing a bell. After a few repetitions, the reaction was produced by the ringing of the bell, without the tasting stimulus. Many human fears, aversions, likes and dislikes are produced in accordance with this principle. We learn to dislike persons in whose presence we have been made to feel humiliated, even when our reason tells us they were not to blame. The objects which we associated with our strong emotional experiences tend to acquire the power of evoking the reaction with which they have become associated.

A fifth method is by securing a new response to a new situation by way of an old emotion. Colvin and Bagley call this process "the sublimation of instinct." (*Human Behavior*, pp. 150 ff.) "This is what has happened, for example, when we 'stand up for what is right,' (or) 'fight for a principle . . .' The cause for which we fight becomes in effect a part of our own personality. We have appropriated it; it is ours. Hence the feelings and emotions which naturally go with the fighting instinct come to attach to the cause that we have made our own if the cause is invaded, questioned, or made light of by others. But while the feeling of resentment is aroused by the invasion of our cause, the primitive method of expressing this feeling must . . . also be modified. . . The Boy Scout movement (as it has been developed in America) makes . . . use of the feelings connected with several of the primitive instincts, attaching them to other objects and assuring responses that are only symbolic of the actual primitive responses."

If the principle be accepted that the great emotional drives may become attached by educational methods to entirely different objects from those which originally evoke their response, the next step in the solution of our main problem will be to determine whether such objects may be generalized notions or ideas. In other words, can an emotion become attached to a general idea as readily as to a more specific object of attention; and if so, will such a generalized idea serve as an effective stimulus in evoking an emotional drive and its concomitant motor response?

A reasonable assumption is that the acquired drives or motive powers will not differ in this respect from the inherited drives. If the inherited drives are both general and special in their adaptations, the acquired drives may also be assumed to be both general and special. Now it is a fact that the instincts are highly generalized, both on the side of the stimuli which will set them off, and on the side of the responsive adaptations which they are able to evoke. The so-called capacities are adaptations to the more special features of the environment. It is also true that the instinctive adaptations more often perform the consummatory, while the capacities perform the preparatory functions. It is reasonable to believe, therefore, that strong emotional drives can become attached to generalized ideas, and that they can be made sufficiently powerful to break down any specific tendencies, whether inherited or acquired, that may interfere with their reaction. An instinct will act *somehow*, and will set up habits in its service. When by the grafting of an idea upon an instinct an ideal is formed, it is reasonable to expect that this ideal will press existing harmonious habits into its service, will break up habits which are contrary to its spirit, and will cause the formation of such new habits as are necessary in the satisfaction of its own imperious demands.

"Ideals dominate large adjustments," says Bagley. "Their intellectual content is often simple; the emotional factor is the important one." They are thus analogous in several respects to the instincts, which also dominate large adjustments, which have relatively little intellectual content, and in which the emotional element is the dominant one. But there are still other points of analogy. Ideals and instincts supply aims and purposes; they may be said to dominate purposes, while knowledge serves to guide, and habit serves to facilitate their accomplishment. The instincts are nature's selection of "virtues," those reactions which have in the history of the race proved serviceable in the struggle for existence; the ideals are man's selection of virtues, "wrought out of the race experience through centuries of struggle and suffering." The instincts are the great stabilizers of natural behavior, holding the conduct of men true to the type that succeeded in maintaining the existence of the race; the ideals are the great stabilizers of society, "holding the conduct of men true to the type that social experience has found to be most effective in maintaining social stability."

Instincts and ideals sometimes run parallel. Many a man who dislikes hard work overcomes his dislike by the ideal of earning money, or because of his desire of gratifying his instinct of acquisition. Habits and ideals sometimes run parallel in the same way, as for example, when a man's personal and business loyalties are in entire harmony with his general ideal and attitude of loyalty. Any habit that is not reinforced by an ideal is likely to give way at the slightest change in the situation, as when a soldier boy, who has learned to obey the laws in the camp but who has not formed an ideal of obedience to the laws, violates every regulation as soon as he enters a civilian community where the restraints of camp life are removed. The function of an ideal is very simple when it harmonizes with instinct and habit. It is only when an ideal runs counter to immediate desires and direct personal gratification, that its function in the guidance of conduct becomes of supreme importance in the moral life.

"It is through [the] pushing forward of the instinct—[the] delayed gratification—that the first . . . step is made toward . . . the conquest of immediate desire. But education must not content itself with conquests that reach no further than this . . . . Other ideas, unconnected with instincts, must be endowed with feeling and thus given strength to overcome immediate tendencies. The [individual] must come in time to work steadfastly at a given problem or a given task, even if a primitive desire is not to be gratified immediately or in the future. In other words, the most effective ideal that man has ever conceived is the one farthest removed from the primitive sanctions. It is the ideal of duty . . . Only when a man works from motives of duty can one depend upon him without question." (Colvin and Bagley, *Human Behavior*, pp. 150 ff.)

But no matter how far the ideals of man may seem to be removed from their original sanctions, the tie which binds them to nature is never severed. In the highest sense of the word, they are natural. "Ideals are kith and kin of man's original hungers and thirsts and cravings," says Thorndike. (*Educational Psychology*, Vol. I, pp. 310-12.) "There is a warfare of man's ideals with his original tendencies, but his ideals themselves came at some time from original yearnings in some man. . . . The impersonal wants, the cravings for truth, beauty and justice, the zeal for competence in workmanship, and the spirit of good will toward men . . . seem far removed from his original proclivities. They *are* remote in the sense that the forces in their favor have to work diligently and ingeniously in order to make them even partial aims for even a minority of men. But in a deeper sense they reside within man himself."

The driving power of an ideal can be explained in terms of natural laws, and especially of the law of effect. When men will sacrifice their present convenience and success, when they will deny themselves of wealth, fame, comfort, position and of many other goods that the world holds dear, and accept poverty, disgrace, suffering and ostracism in the service of an ideal of honor or duty, it is because they wish to accomplish an end which seems to them highly desirable of accomplishment, and because they find greater satisfaction in the pursuit of their ideal than in present ease and comfort. The boy who learns to play fair in a game instead of taking unfair advantage does so because he finds greater shame in being dishonorable than in being defeated, or because he finds greater satisfaction in the consciousness of being honorable than in the hope of victory. The ideal which he has set for himself is his *standard* of conduct, and to fall below his standard would give him greater annoyance than any other pain could give; for it would mean failure in the realization of himself. He has learned to feel, by means of some overwhelming experience, that his standard is exceedingly worth while. This subjective appreciation is incapable of accepting outside valuations. For each individual, *his* ideals are absolute. The things he appreciates, the things he loves, *must* be worth while. The strength of the appreciation is limited only by the individual's emotional capacity.

The presence of so imperious a subjective element in the mind would in itself create a state of tension something akin to hunger or thirst. An unrealized ideal is a want, a need, the failure to satisfy which arouses a feeling of irritation and annoyance, and acts as a powerful consummatory drive. An unrealized ideal with its vague longings and feelings of uneasiness, is a subjective element of great potentiality. Its very existence implies a high type of intellectual and moral development, with a capacity for selection and constructive imagination. It is doubly under the influence of the law of effect; for it is not only driven by annoyance of the present and the past, but is also drawn by anticipation of the future.

When an ideal has become more or less habitual, it is called an attitude. The attitude is a mind "set" in a certain direction. It thus becomes a mechanism as well as a drive. Its advantage in the control of conduct lies in the fact that the mind "set" directs the power of selective attention. An individual will see what he elects to see in any situation. The mind "set" screens out what one does not attend to, what one does not want. A trustworthiness mind "set" with its accompanying desire to live up to one's responsibilities, reduces the chances of yielding to the temptation to lie, cheat, steal, and do poor work. One is looking for something else and finds what he is looking for.

The assumption that ideals and attitudes perform a powerful function in the control of conduct is entirely in harmony with the opinion of the world's best thinkers, with the known laws of nature, and with the laws of learning. The actual demonstration of their function, however, must needs be left to experimentation.

CHAPTER V

AN EXPERIMENT

The solution which has been offered under the discussion of Chapter IV is hypothetical. The proof must be obtained by means of experiment.

In arranging for this experiment it was decided to choose groups of boys rather than groups of girls, for the reason that the organization of groups of boys has been carried on far more extensively than the organization of groups of girls, and also for the practical reason that Mr. James E. West, chief executive of the Boy Scouts of America, offered the use of several Boy Scout troops for experimental purposes. Only one group of girls was tested, Group F.

In addition to the two experimental groups, it was decided to make use of two control groups. One of the experimental groups is located in New York City, the other in Elizabeth, New Jersey. One of the control groups is located in New York City, the other in Brooklyn, New York. The attempt was made to secure four groups of about the same intelligence and of about the same home and neighborhood environment. A comparison of the intelligence quotients given in the tables will show to what extent the first attempt succeeded. It is believed that the home environment of the four groups is about on a par, with the exception of Group E, which seems to live in a superior environment. Special training was arranged for the two experimental groups, and it was agreed that no special training would be given the control groups between the time of the first and the second series of tests.

It was decided to make the ideal of trustworthiness the objective of the training. The reason for this choice is the fact that trustworthiness is the first and one of the most fundamental ideals that are taught to the Boy Scouts. Every good Scout leader attempts to teach trustworthiness, although every leader does not emphasize this ideal as perhaps it was emphasized by the two leaders of the experimental groups during the duration of this experiment. It is believed that similar results would have been obtained if the ideal of loyalty, or perhaps the ideal of service had been chosen as the objective of the training.

The methods of training used with the experimental groups were such as are commonly used by the leaders of the Boy Scout troops, modified to fit the principles which are assumed in Chapter III of this study, and with special emphasis placed upon the ideal of trustworthiness. The time of training was about three months, but the time elapsed between the first and the second series of tests was only about seven weeks. The reason for this difference is the fact that it was found impracticable to test the boys until they had been brought somewhat under the control of the leader. It is not likely that the results of the first tests would have been greatly different from what they were had it been practicable to give them at the very beginning of the organization of the two groups.

It is not believed that the maximum results can be secured in so short a period of time; however, the point at issue is not the amount of improvement that can be secured, but whether there is any improvement at all. Every precaution was taken by the experimenter to secure proper test conditions, and every effort was made by the Scout leaders to carry out their part of the program.

The experimenter had nothing to do with the actual training of the two groups. He held a series of conferences with the leaders and finally gave each of them a copy of a digest of the principles which are assumed to hold true in social education, and which are enumerated in Chapter III of this study.

The following letters from the two leaders give clear and detailed outlines of the methods which were followed in the training of both groups. As may be gathered from these letters, the devices and methods used were the products of the initiative and originality of the leaders. It is not likely that there is any special efficacy in these devices and methods. The success which the two leaders achieved was undoubtedly due to their ability to create an effective group spirit among the boys, and to direct this spirit by tactful suggestion toward moral ends. The strength and enthusiasm of the leaders, their ability to inspire loyalty among their followers, were probably greater factors in producing the results than were the devices and methods which they used.

BOY SCOUTS OF AMERICA
Headquarters National Council
The Fifth Avenue Building
New York City

April 27, 1920

Mr. Paul F. Voelker
Teachers College
Columbia University
New York City

Dear Mr. Voelker:

In compliance with your request, I am glad to make the following statements in regard to my work with my group of Scouts:

The group was organized in January, the boys whom you tested joining the group that month or very early in February. I have been working with these boys up to the time of your second test on April 22, approximately three months. During this time I have been meeting with them weekly. On four Saturdays I have had a hike or a meeting, at which a part of all of these boys were present. Part of them have also been at my office a few times for instruction in First Aid.

The work has been carried to a considerable extent along the lines suggested in your analysis transmitted in your letter of March 12th, 1920, on the opportunities, methods, and devices of social education. Taking your 12 points in order:

I. *Social Education Can Best Be Given in a Social Environment.*

Scout work is, of course, founded on the "gang" as a unit. I have endeavored to develop a sense of group consciousness.

(*a*) I have on several occasions talked to the boys, telling them of my hopes for the development of a strong troop and urging them to do everything possible for the welfare of the troop.

(*b*) I have encouraged intensive preparation for the entering of an inter-troop field meeting, which is shortly to be held, in order that the troop might make the best possible showing on that occasion.

(*c*) We have held an entertainment for the raising of Camp funds, the purpose of which is for the use of the entire troop in camping together, and have stimulated, so far as possible, activity on the part of all in the sale of tickets for the mutual good of the troop.

II. *Social Standards Should Be Built Up Within the Group and Not Imposed from Without.*

The voluntary observance of the Scout Law and Oath by the Scout, crystallizes the gang code of ethics. The boys are urged to adopt the Scout code as the gang code. The boys have been encouraged, so far as possible, to develop their own application of the code. Thus, in the case of a boy who did not prove sufficiently loyal to the group to maintain his activity, and who dropped out, but later applied for re-admission, the boys were given an opportunity to discuss the matter themselves and to decide on what action should be taken. In this case they decided that he had not been loyal to the troop, and therefore should not be re-admitted, and they voted into the troop in his place a boy of much less promising appearance.

III. *Every Modification of the Group Standards and Every Moral Readjustment in the Minds of the Members of the Group Can Best Be Brought About by Grappling with Vital Issues.*

The working out of this principle is illustrated in the particular instance listed above, concerning the re-admission of a boy who has not proven loyal to the troop.

IV. *The Principle of Social Participation.*

The discussion of the instance previously mentioned and decision reached by the troop illustrates this principle also. Considerable emphasis is placed in the work of the troop on team activities. Thus many of the contests have been team contests of patrol versus patrol. Again, in the preparation for the inter-troop field meeting which is to be held, considerable training of different phases have been given with teams of four to eight boys training together. In the exhibition given by the troop the boys themselves explained to the audience what they were doing and why.

V. *The Principle of Group Motivation.*

The emphasis laid, as previously explained, on patrol and troop activities constantly utilizes this principle by placing stress upon the welfare of the whole group.

VI. *The Small Group Virtues Should Be Strengthened First.*

An inter-patrol contest was started on the night that the troop organized,— has been running almost continuously since. This has already developed a splendid patrol spirit. The troop as a unit will come into contact and competition with other troops shortly, and preparations for these contests are developing a corresponding spirit. Thus, the small group is being developed first.

VII. *The Small Group, as Soon as Its Virtues Have Been Strengthened So That the Leader Can Depend upon Them, Shall Be Thrown into Contact with Other Groups.*

I have also given several illustrations of how this is being done in the troop.

VIII. *The Development of the Large Group Virtues Should Be Based upon the Small Group Virtues.*

This is continuously done in Scouting, as the same activities and the same Law and Oath apply for the large group as for the small group.

IX. *Define the Limits and the Conflicts between the Small and the Large Group Relationships.*

Throughout the work, by suggestions here and there the things which are common between different groups are being emphasized rather than the differences and emphasis is constantly followed by suggestions to the fact that the principles of Scouting apply to a Scout's relation to all others as well as his relation to other Scouts. The various contests, etc., on the other hand define the limits of each group.

X. *The Principle of Utilizing Mottoes, Slogans, Shibboleths, Taboos and Other Words or Phrases Which Will Tend to Unify or Organize for Each Individual the Standards Which He is Accepting from the Group.*

Scout work is of course full of such phrases, e. g.; "Do a Good Turn Daily"; "Be Prepared"; "A Scout is Trustworthy"; and "Once a Scout—Always a Scout."

XI. *The Law of Annoyance.*

There has really been no serious case of discipline to make an application of this. However, in the case of one boy who caused some distrubance while I was talking, the patrol received one demerit in the inter-patrol contest. This served not only to make the boy realize his error, but it brought on him the displeasure of the other boys in a way which was very effective in stopping further disorder.

The boys also were given the Self-Analysis Test developed by you.

XII. *The Law of Satisfaction.*

I have, on several occasions, taken pains to compliment a boy on some piece of good work that he had done, or in talking to his parents to speak favorably to them of his work. Again, in cases where the Scout reflected credit to the group in his contact with someone outside the troop, I have commented favorably on the incident to the troop (without naming the individual).

. . . .

Aside from the above I have endeavored to develop trustworthiness in the Scouts in two ways:

(a) By repeated suggestions as to the importance and significance of the Scout Oath and Law, and of the value of living up to them.

(b) By specifically emphasizing to them the law stating "A Scout is Trustworthy."

Among other occasions in which this has been done, have been as follows:

(a) On February 13th I told a story in which one man was trustworthy and another was not.

(b) Later in the same day I cautioned them to be trustworthy in a game which they were playing.

(c) On March 12th, in speaking of plans for a hike, I emphasized the importance of trustworthiness on the hike.

(d) On April 9th I complimented a boy on a report received from another scout official that he had been trustworthy in performance of assigned duties.

(e) On or about April 20th, in writing to the Scouts urging them to attend your second examination, I wrote out to the Scouts stating that I had given my word that each of the boys would be present, and charging each boy on his Scout Honor to be present, unless circumstances beyond his control prevented it.

I do not by any means think I have reached the limit in the development of these boys, but know that I have made a beginning. I intend to work along the lines already indicated.

I find a much greater response than at the start to suggestions made; a much better discipline; a much greater group loyalty; a much more reliable response to tasks imposed.

On numerous occasions I have found that of late when I have assigned tasks to a boy to fulfill, I have been much more certain of getting satisfactory results than I was in the first few weeks.

I did nothing to put the boys on their guard against the tests.

Very sincerely yours,
(Signed) C. A. EDSON.

MR. PAUL F. VOELKER
Teachers College
Columbia University
New York City

DEAR MR. VOELKER:

I have held your letter of April 24th so that I could give some thought to the questions you bring to my attention, as I deem these matters very important in their relation to the scout movement. It is fine to know that you believe the tests are working out as you expected they would. Certainly the time and attention you gave the work should be rewarded by success.

1. *How Long Have You Trained These Boys?*

I started the middle of January and have been meeting once a week up to the present time.

2. *What Did You Do Especially to Try to Make Them More Trustworthy?*

Explained thoroughly the tenderfoot requirements. These contain the basic principles upon which the Scout Movement is built.

Gave a detailed explanation of the oath. Pointed out the results which would follow the failure of the President of the United States to live up to his oath.

Told short stories of our country's heroes, bringing out the points of the Scout Law.

An opportunity of driving home important points was presented by a boy who insisted on keeping on his hat in the club house which is against the rules unless a scout is in full uniform. He was suspended by the director of the club for a week. It was decided between the director and myself to deny the boy entrance to the club to attend the meeting. He sat in the gutter in front of the building during the time the meeting was in progress. I took no notice of him but at the next meeting I spoke about his surly attitude, also explained it was not only a reflection upon himself but the troop. I indicated that perhaps after all my leadership was not what it should be or certainly during two months of association he should have learned to act like a gentleman. This scout was also advised he owed loyalty to the group and that a boy was not trustworthy who takes an oath to live up to fine ideals and which had been thoroughly explained to him; then proceeds to allow a feeling of spitefulness make him forget himself.

3. *What Methods Do You Think Are the Best?*

To develop first of all the enthusiasm of the boy for the movement by making the meetings as attractive as possible; inspire confidence in himself, and others in the group and the leader. We challenged another troop to competitive games requiring knot-tying and in which, if one boy failed to tie the knot properly, the others were thrown into confusion. The troop competed against was well established while our troop was in its third week. Our group won. Instantly a spirit of confidence in each other seemed to take hold. They realized they had been taught quickly and effectively and showed much greater confidence in the leader and in those whom the latter brought in to aid.

A boy when he feels he is taking an important part in the activities of the troop will be more inclined to act in unison with the group.

I have tried to control the boys through suggestions but have kept in the background as much as possible allowing one of the older boys who was elected by the group to carry on the affairs of the troop with my advice and help.

4. *Have You Reached the Limit with These Boys or Can You Do More for Them?*

The work is only begun, really the foundation is not yet completed.

5. *What More Can You Do?*

Give the boy a loftier viewpoint of things of life by bringing him into intimate contact with the things of nature through the scouting program.

6. *What Evidence Have You in the Way of Things You Hear Them Say and See Them Do, that They Are Improving?*

It is hard to judge one's own work. Scout Executive Geddes said that the club's superintendent told him that there was a vast improvement in the boys' manners, and especially in the club the second week we had met. If you will recall, they were very hard to control the first night we went in there, but after that time they showed a vast improvement especially in obeying when they were spoken to and in following out directions. After the third week when I went into the meeting room a chair and a table had been placed for my convenience and other chairs had been arranged around the room as I had instructed they should be at a previous meeting. I had not asked for the table however. Certainly their attitude, toward things brought up in the meeting, has been changed and there seems to be no more of the bickering and arguing which used to manifest itself.

7. *Did You Do Anything to Put Them on Guard Against These Tests?*

Absolutely nothing to my knowledge.

It should be taken into consideration that some of the original boys were not only in the older boy stage, but they were sons of parents who couldn't read nor write the English language. It is not easy to change their attitude to a standard of things which had been foreign to them. One boy wanted to stick to me and attended the meetings. His parents wouldn't allow him to be a scout. I offered to explain the program to them but the boy said it was useless, they couldn't understand.

It has been a great pleasure to associate with you and have this small part in helping establish the facts in connection with your main thesis.

Yours very sincerely,

(Signed) WALLACE L. NEILL.

The first step of the experiment was to provide a means of measuring trustworthiness. It was decided not to try any tests of moral discrimination such as were used by Miss Bronner in 1913 in her study of delinquent girls, for the reason, as was shown rather conclusively in her study, that high moral discrimination does not necessarily insure high moral conduct. Discrimination tests are really tests of intelligence. To serve the ends of this experiment, moral tests were needed. In other words, not the intelligence, but the purpose of the individual and his ability to carry out his purpose were to be measured. It was decided that the tests must confront the individual with real, not imaginary, situations; that the only way to learn whether a boy will steal is to give him the opportunity. To be sure, each test is but a random sampling of an individual's trustworthiness; but as the number of cases is increased, the chances of error due to the random sampling may be gradually reduced.

One of the difficulties connected with the invention of these tests, was the creation of actual situations. Some of the critics of the tests have maintained that it is morally wrong to create such situations and present them to the boys for reaction. In reply it may be said that sooner or later life will present all of these temptations. Our efforts to improve the moral conduct of the boys should at least counterbalance any culpability that might be attached to our placing temptation in their way. It has been urged by one of our critics that the testing of the boys should be done by means of scientific observation,—that a boy should be followed for a period of days, weeks, or months, and carefully observed under all conditions and all situations, to see how he would respond. This suggestion is utterly impracticable. If a trained observer could be found who would "shadow" a boy for a period of time it is doubtful whether he would not soon be detected by the boy. Moreover, how could this trained observer, or anyone else, guarantee that the boy during this period of time would confront every situation that we were able to present to him in the series of tests? From the standpoint of expediency alone, the tests are more desirable than the proposed scheme of observation of random reactions.

It seemed practicable to use the method of trial and error in order to find out whether our tests would prove successful. Many of the tests fell by the wayside because they were either too crude or too palpably evident. Among these tests may be mentioned the following.

The Puzzle Test

Can the subject be trusted not to steal an object which appeals to his interest and his cupidity?

DIRECTIONS: Place a box full of puzzles upon a small table. Scatter a few of the puzzles in careless fashion around the box and on the floor. Request the subject to try to solve some of them. Leave him alone for a few minutes. When you return ask him how many he has solved.

Dismiss the subject and count the puzzles.

There is no doubt that these puzzles were attractive and interesting to the boys, and that perhaps under other circumstances an occasional boy would have appropriated one or two of the puzzles, but for some reason no boy ever took a puzzle from the desk of his examiner. It may be that he feared detection. It may be that he had formed a strong inhibition against taking property from a school or church building. At any rate it could not be considered a good test as long as everyone was able to pass it perfectly.

Another test which was eliminated after trial was the "Lost Article Test."

Lost Article Test

Can the subject be trusted to make a sincere effort to return a lost article to its owner?

DIRECTIONS: Send the subject on an errand through a long hall in the building. Make sure that there shall be no passers-by during the interval of the test. Place a pocketbook on the floor of the hall in a conspicuous place where the subject will be sure to see it. The pocketbook should contain some small change, a key, several theatre ticket checks, and a card bearing the pocketbook owner's name and address; also a small sealed envelope marked "important." The owner should be a person unknown to the subject. Make sure after the subject has returned from his errand that the pocketbook has been taken. Make no mention of the incident at this time or later.

SCORING: If the subject returns the pocketbook with all its contents to the examiner or to the owner, score him 10. If he removes part of the contents and returns the rest, score him in proportion to the value of the property returned. Count the small envelope as of three times the value of the money, and the key as half the value of the money.

This test probably failed for the same reason that the puzzle test failed. The situation was too hazardous to produce a real temptation.

Another test which was not found successful was the "Duck on the Rock Test."

Duck on the Rock Test

Can the subject be trusted not to cheat in a game?

Each player is provided with a stone called a "duck" about the size of a baseball. A large rock or post is chosen as the duck rock, and twenty-five feet from it a throwing line is drawn. On this duck rock one player places his duck and stands by it as guard. This guard is selected at the outset by all of the players throwing their ducks at the duck rock from the throwing line. The one whose duck falls nearest to the rock becomes the first guard. The other players stand behind the throwing line and take turns in throwing at the guard's duck on the rock with their stones, trying to knock it from the rock. After each throw a player must recover his own duck and run back home beyond the throwing line. Should he be tagged by the guard while trying to do this, he must change places with the guard. The guard may tag him at any time when he is within the throwing line, unless he stands with his foot on his own duck where it first fell. He may stand in this way as long as necessary, awaiting an opportunity to run home; but the moment he lifts his duck from the ground, or takes his foot from it, he may be tagged by the guard. Having once lifted his duck to run home with it, a player may not again place it on the ground.

The guard may not tag any player unless his own duck be on the rock. Before he may chase the thrower, he must therefore pick up his own duck and replace it should it have been knocked off. This replacing gives the thrower an opportunity to recover his own duck and run home; but should the duck not have been displaced from the duck rock, the thrower may have to wait either at a safe distance or with his foot on his own duck if he can get to it, until some other thrower has displaced the duck on the rock, and so engaged the time and attention of the guard. Several players may thus be waiting at once to recover their ducks, some of them near the duck rock with a foot on their ducks, others at a distance. Any player tagged by the guard must change places with him, placing his own duck on the rock. The guard must quickly recover his duck and run for the throwing line after tagging a player, as he in turn may be tagged as soon as the new guard has placed his duck on the rock.

A stone that falls very near the duck rock without displacing the duck may also prove disastrous to the thrower. Should a stone fall within a hand span (stretching from finger tip to the thumb) of the duck rock without knocking off the duck, the guard challenges the thrower by shouting "Span!", whereupon he proceeds to measure with his hand the distance between the duck rock and the stone. Should the distance be as he surmises, the thrower of the stone has to change places with him, put his own duck on the rock, and become the guard. This rule cultivates expert throwers.

When used in a gymnasium, this game must be played with bean bags, in which case one bag may be balanced on top of an Indian club for the duck on the rock.

OPPORTUNITIES FOR CHEATING:

1. Picking up duck before distance is measured in order not to become guard.
2. Playing out of turn.
3. Taking foot off duck and then putting it on again in order not to be caught.
4. Stepping over line for advantage in throwing.

INSTRUCTIONS TO PLAYERS: The teacher or leader of the game must take pains to explain that certain advantages must not be taken by some players which are not to be taken by others. Every game must have "rules" and to get the most out of a game the rules must be obeyed. When this game is used as a test for trustworthiness, there should not be an umpire; the players should be left to their own devices.

METHOD OF SCORING: The examiner should be in the guise of a spectator. He must give his attention to one player at a time. He must follow this player through at least six rounds in order to obtain a fair score.

Since there are four opportunities to cheat in each round, in six rounds there would be 24 opportunities. If the player takes advantage of half of them, his score will be 50 per cent. Care must be taken to make sure that the "error" was not accidental.

Undoubtedly this test can be made successful when there is

a sufficient number of trained workers so that each boy in the game may be closely observed. Possibly a simpler game test could be found in which attempts to cheat would be more evident.

Another test which was discarded was the "Memory Test."

Memory Test

Can the subject be trusted not to cheat in an examination?

Each subject is handed a copy of Edgar A. Guest's poem "The Tramp," with the request that he memorize it and bring it with him to the next meeting. Explain to the subject that the test will be to see how much he can write of the poem without looking at the copy. Immediately before the test each subject is requested to read the poem once more. A fresh copy is handed to any who neglected to bring theirs with them. Each subject is then directed to put the poem in his pocket and is given pencil and paper for the test. A time limit is announced and the examiner finds occasion to leave the room.

The original copies are collected along with the pencils and test papers.

At the next meeting each subject is supplied with a copy of the same poem, and he is given another opportunity to read it through. The copies are then collected and the test is repeated without previous warning. During this trial the examiner does not leave the room. If any subject has cheated during the first test, the fact will be revealed in the second test.

A score may be obtained by dividing the percentage of words written in the second test by the percentage of words written in the first test.

This test was not followed up because of the impracticability of demanding that the boys commit the poem to memory. The demand could well be made by a teacher but not by an outsider who was merely coming in to give the boys a test. It is still believed that the memory test may prove to be helpful if used in connection with school work.

After considerable experimentation it was found that certain tests were successful to the extent of not being passed by all the students. Occasionally all the members of the same group would secure a perfect rating in one of the tests. This was probably due to the fact that all the individuals had been trained in that particular response.

The following tests were used in the first part of the experiment. They are referred to hereafter as Series I.

Series I of the Tests

1. The Overstatement Test

Can the subject be trusted to refuse credit that is not due him?

DIRECTIONS: Some time during the day, and if possible just before the group test is given, all persons to be examined are called together by their teacher or leader and given marks in some subject.

When the student comes to the examiner for this test, the following questions are put to him:

1. What is your name? Your age? In what grade are you?
2. Do you like school (or Scouting)?
3. What study do you like best?
4. I understand that you are good in geography. (Or mention some other subject in which he does his best work.) Is it easy for you?
5. Do I understand that you are above the average in language? or, Did you receive 95 in arithmetic in your last examination?

(The mark suggested is an overstatement. Care should be taken to mention only subjects in which students have recently been marked, also to choose subjects in which no student is perfect.)

SCORING: The subject scores 0 if he nods, is silent, or says yes. He scores 10 if he contradicts the examiner and gives his correct grades. If he attempts to modify the overstatement only slightly (as some subjects do) he is given credit in proportion to the amount of the modification, being rated between 0 and 10.

2. THE M AND N TEST OF SUGGESTIBILITY

(An adaptation from Miss June Downey's *Will Profile*.)

Can the subject be trusted to stick to a point when he knows he is right?

DIRECTIONS: One of the examiners holds up two envelopes and says: "Here are two envelopes containing instructions for two different mental tests. One test is very easy, the other is hard. You may choose which envelope you will open." After giving instructions the examiner holds the two envelopes labelled in heavy print "M" and "N" in front of the subject, "N" always to the right. When the subject has made his choice one of the examiners records on a slip of paper the letter on the envelope that the subject did not choose.

(Interval.)

The examiner says, "Now we will take up the test in the envelope. Which one did you choose?"

Suggestion A: "Are you sure?" "Wasn't it————" (Name the other letter. Record answer verbatim and manner.)

Suggestion B: "I made a record of your choice. I'll see what it says. It says————" (Again name the letter NOT chosen. Record subject's answer and manner. Give plenty of time, as the final reaction may be somewhat different from the immediate one; or the subject may not say anything at all at first.)

Suggestion C: "Do you think I made a mistake?" (Record answer. All suggestions should be given in as matter-of-fact way as possible. At close say, "Never mind, we'll omit this test.")

A few subjects forget the chosen envelope and a few others notice position to right or left rather than letter. If so, contradiction of the remembered position or letter can still be made.

SCORING: Score the subject 1 to 10 points as follows:

10. Burden of proof thrown on examiner. Spontaneous suggestion of examiner's error. Or angry or suspicious reaction.
9. Burden of proof thrown on examiner. Examiner's error asserted positively.

8. Logically positive; reasons cited for assurance; subject assumes the burden of proof; asserts examiner's error when asked with, usually, a reiteration of his reasons for confidence.
7. Positive, but won't argue; mild reaction to C, either an assertion of his own accuracy or gentle assertion of examiner's error.
6. Non-committal, typical remark at C: "I don't know," or baffled attitude at C. Can't reconcile the discrepancy. Typical remark: "You ought to know if you made a record, but I have a good memory."
5. Conciliatory: Explains how mistake was made. "You may have misunderstood me." "I may have told you wrong."
4. Indifferent: Unconvinced but non-resistant. "Well, whichever you say." "I won't contradict." "It doesn't make any difference." Or an evasive reaction; when question is asked, examinee changes the subject.
3. Admits doubt at C.
2. Admits doubt at B. Typical remarks: "I may have made a mistake." "That's queer!"
1. Gives in at suggestion B. Typical remark: "That fooled me that time." Or gives in at suggestion A. Or envelope forgotten.

3. Let-Me-Help-You Test

Can the subject be trusted to refuse help in the solution of a puzzle when he has been instructed to try to solve it independently?

DIRECTIONS: The subject is given two puzzles as follows:

No. 1. The Square Puzzle

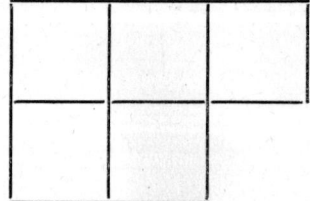

An Experiment

Fifteen toothpicks are placed on the table so as to form five equal squares, as in the figure. Remove three toothpicks so as to leave three such squares only.

No. 2. THE MATCH PUZZLE

```
1111
     111      111      111
     111               111
     111      111      111
```

The 1's represent matches. The problem is to keep the same number of groups of matches (8) in the figure, and to redistribute them in such a way that the 4 matches outside the figure may be added without adding to the sum of matches (9) on each side of the figure.

If the subject cannot solve the puzzles, give him a drawing of them and request him to put the drawing in his pocket. Ask him to agree not to receive help from anyone. Give him three days' time to work out the solutions, and promise to give him credit if he brings in the correct solutions within that time.

One puzzle is sufficient if none of the subjects are familiar with it. Other puzzles may be added when this test is given to a group of advanced students, or where there is a likelihood that some of the puzzles may be known to certain members of the group.

(Interval.)

When the subject appears for his individual tests, the second examiner (who was not present at the assignment of the puzzles) opens a box of the Gilbert puzzles (consisting of the Twin Rings Puzzle, The Question Puzzle, The Three Rings Puzzle, The Shamrock Puzzle, The Nail Puzzle, and the Conjuring Rings Puzzle) and says:

"I have some puzzles here for you. Did Mr.———— (naming the chief examiner) give you any puzzles? Could you do them? What were they? These are easy. Shall I show you?" The subject's replies are carefully recorded.

The examiner leaves the subject alone for a time to give him opportunity to solve the Gilbert Puzzles. The object of this part of the test is to make the test interesting and make the offer of help appear to be casual. Incidentally, the subject is given opportunity to appropriate one of the puzzles if he desires, and to "find" a small pocketbook which has been placed under a chair.

SCORING: The subjects who accept help are scored zero. Those who refuse help are scored ten. Those who partially yield to the temptation to receive help are scored in proportion to the amount of their yielding.

If a subject finds the pocketbook and fails to turn it over to the examiner or to the Lost and Found Department of the school, or if he appropriates one or more of the puzzles, he is given a demerit.

4. BORROWING ERRAND TEST

Can the subject be trusted to return borrowed property according to promise?

DIRECTIONS: Request the subject to run an errand. He is to go to a designated address and ask to borrow a pamphlet of Mr. Blank (who is one of the examiner's assistants). When the subject arrives, Mr. Blank says, "Yes, I will let you have the pamphlet if you will promise to return it before 9 o'clock tomorrow morning." Each pamphlet is marked with a key number so that the subjects who return the pamphlet may receive proper credit.

When the subject returns with the pamphlet, the examiner thanks him and places the pamphlet on the table without other comment. If the subject says, "I must return the pamphlet before 9 o'clock tomorrow morning," the examiner says, "Very well; I will have it here for you; call for it before you leave."

SCORING: Score the subject 10 points if he returns the pamphlet; score him zero if he fails to return it.

5. PURCHASING ERRAND TEST

Can the subject be trusted not to accept overchange?

DIRECTIONS: The subject is handed a card on which is written his own name and the words, "One copy of opposites test, nine cents." The examiner hands him a twenty-five cent piece and requests him to go to the neighboring stationery store to purchase a copy of the test.

When the subject arrives at the store, the examiner's confederate takes the card, hands out an envelope containing the test and says "Nine cents, please." When the subject hands her the twenty-five cent piece, she carelessly hands him two dimes, one nickel and one cent.

If the subject immediately returns the ten cents overcharge to the clerk, she thanks him and records the fact on the card. If he brings twenty-six cents to the examiner, the latter says: "Did I not give you twenty-five cents?" If the subject says "yes" the examiner says: "Did you put some of your own money in with this?"

SCORING: If the subject returns the change to the clerk, or if on returning all the money to the examiner he insists that none of it is his own, he is scored 10. If he keeps the overchange he is scored zero.

6. THE TIP TEST

Can the subject be trusted not to accept a tip for a trifling courtesy?

Tipping is a debasing custom which either flatters or protects the vanity of the giver and debases the self-respect of the receiver. It is contrary to the rules of the Boy Scouts and the Camp Fire Girls to receive tips.

DIRECTIONS: When the subject returns from one of his errands (care should be taken that it is but a short distance) the examiner thanks him and offers him a tip for his courtesy.

SCORING: The subject is scored zero if he accepts the tip; he is scored 10 if he refuses it.

7. THE PUSH BUTTON TEST

Can the subject be trusted to do a given task exactly as it was given to him to do?

DIRECTIONS: This test requires two watches and an electric bell. The bell, which rings in response to pressure on a push button, must be in a room sufficiently distant so as not to be heard by the subject. The two watches must be synchronized.

The subject is seated in a chair near the push button. He is given a watch and told to push the button every two minutes, when the second hand is exactly at 60, until told to stop. The examiner's assistant, with the other watch, keeps an exact record of the ringing of the bell. The examiner leaves the subject to himself for ten minutes.

Interesting and diverting objects are left in the room, so that the subject, unless he is quite trustworthy, may be tempted to leave the assigned task.

This test may be varied by having the subject turn light on and off, or off and on as directed, the examiner observing the light through the transom in another room. Or, an automatic time recording device may be used.

SCORING: If the subject records the time accurately within three seconds he is given two points for that period. Five perfect records during the period of ten minutes will give him a score of ten. Each one he misses will subtract two points from the ten. Failure to push the button within three seconds of the required time is scored the same as complete failure for that period.

8. "A" TEST
(Suggested by Dr. E. L. Thorndike)

Can the subject be trusted to work faithfully at an assigned task when there are other interests to distract him?

DIRECTIONS: Instruct the subject to count all the a's that he can count during a period of 5 minutes. Use printed material in which he is not likely to be interested. Record the count.

Next instruct him to count all the a's that he can count in an illustrated picture book during the same length of time. Again record the count.

The test should disclose the effect of the distraction of the pictures.

The print should be of the same size in both tasks.

SCORING: Divide the number of a's marked during the second exercise by the number of a's marked during the first. The quotient will be the per cent of perfection. Multiply by ten and discard the decimal. The number obtained is the subjects' crude score.

9. THE PROFILE TEST

Can the subject be trusted not to peep when he is placed on his honor to keep his eyes closed?

DIRECTIONS: The Pintner Profile boards are used for this test. The boards vary from the standard only in the detail that the ears are painted and not carved. Each subject is given a board and instructed to dump the profile on the table before him, to shuffle the blocks, and to put them together as rapidly as possible. The examiners watch him in this process and if he experiences any difficulty he is helped in putting the profile together. The object of this part of the performance is to make sure that the boy thoroughly understands how the profile should be put together.

The boys are then requested to repeat the test,—dump the blocks, shuffle them, and put them back in place; this time with eyes closed. They are told that as soon as they think they have a perfect profile they are to open their eyes. If it is found to be perfect the record is to be made on a slip of paper,—"first trial correct"; if there is an error it is to be recorded,—"first trial wrong." The boys have three trials to complete the profile with closed eyes.

The examiner does not verify the completed work. He merely accepts the boy's statement on the written slip.

SCORING: If the subject reports one successful effort, he is scored 7; if he reports two successful efforts, he is scored 3; if he reports three or more successful efforts, he is scored 0. The subject who reports complete failure is scored 10.

This method of scoring is somewhat arbitrary. It will be recalled that the ears in these profile boards are not grooved as they are in the standard Pintner boards, but painted. It is not possible for a subject to tell the top from the bottom side of one of the blocks by the sense of touch alone. However, there is one chance in sixteen that all the blocks will appear in correct position; there is one chance in 256 that all the blocks will appear in correct position in two consecutive trials; and there is one chance in 4096 that all the blocks will appear in correct position in three consecutive trials. If a subject, therefore, claims to have been successful in one trial, there is one chance in 16 that he is telling the truth, and the score of 7 is given as a concession to the possibility that it is the truth. If the examiner could be sure that he is not telling the truth, the score should be 0. When the subject claims that he has been successful in two consecutive trials, there is one chance in 256 that he is telling the truth, and a score of 3 is given instead of a 0. The remoteness of the chance that an individual could be successful in three successive trials without cheating makes the score of 0 seem justifiable under these circumstances.

10. THE TRACING AND OPPOSITES TEST

Can the subject be trusted not to cheat in an examination?

DIRECTIONS: This test is given on a prepared four-page folder, perforated at the fold. Following is a reproduction of page 1:

OPPOSITES TEST

good ....
begin ....
above ....
bottom ....
ancient ....
black ....
sharp ....
if ....
cold ....
alive ....
alike ....
attack ....
clean ....
awake ....
ancestor ....
answer ....
pleasure ....
always ....
advance ....
gladness ....

Your name

An Experiment 79

Pages 2 and 4 are blank. A piece of transparent waxed paper is fastened with a clip at each corner upon page 3, in such manner that the figure and the typed instructions are perfectly legible. Page 3 is as follows:

TRACING TEST

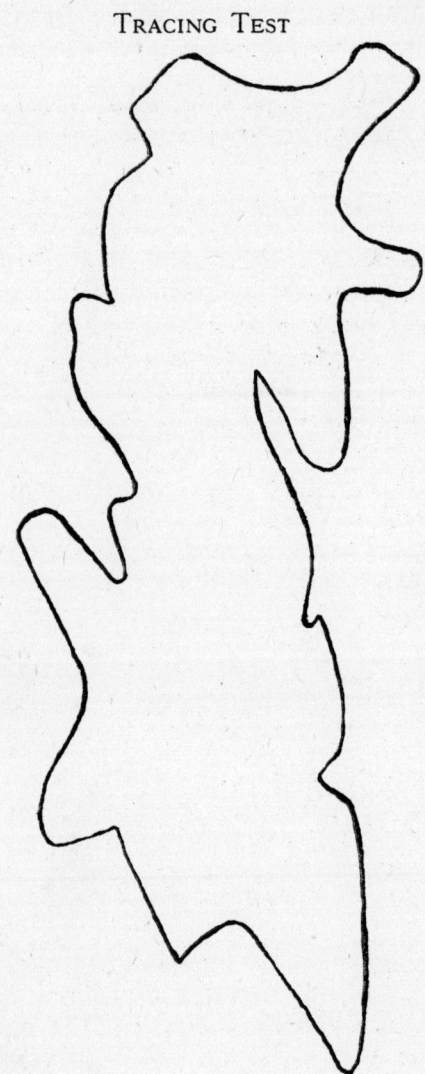

(Trace the figure as carefully as possible.)

The technique of this test is as follows: A folder is placed before each subject with face side (page 1) down, and page 4 (blank) up. At a given signal, the folders are opened and the subjects trace the figure on page 3 according to instructions, one minute being given for this work. When the signal is given to stop, the folder is closed so that page 4 is down and page 1 is up. The subjects are then instructed to write their names at the bottom of the page, and then to write as many opposites as possible within the space of two minutes.

When the time is called, one of the examiners asks for the Tracing Test for the purpose of correction. The *examiners* then proceed to tear off the Tracing Test at the perforation (including the waxed paper which is still attached by means of the clips), the first page being left with the subject. The assistant examiners leave the room at this point, while the chief examiner reads the correct opposites, giving the subjects the opportunity to mark their own papers. Care is taken to create lax conditions during the process of correction, the subjects being encouraged to ask questions. The examiner goes to the window or arranges to have some one call him to the door. The subjects are thus given ample opportunity to cheat.

A comparison of pages 1 and 3 will reveal whether or not the subject attempted to cheat by adding words or making changes during the process of correcting his own paper. The waxed paper will show a perfect tracing of all the words which the subject wrote originally. The examiner, of course, had provided each of his subjects with a hard pencil.

SCORING: The subject scores 10 if he has made no attempt to cheat; he scores 0 if he cheats.

THE ADMINISTRATION OF THE TESTS

The following plan of operation was gradually developed. The group tests were given first. Then the class was left in charge of a teacher or leader while its individual members were called out one by one for the other tests. Each individual was sent by one of the examiners to a nearby store on the purchasing and borrowing errands, and on his return was offered a tip. He was then taken in charge by another examiner for the overstatement test, the last part of the M and N Test, the Pushing-the-Button Test, the last part of the A-Test, and the Let-Me-Help-You Test. Sometimes one examiner could keep two subjects at work, one of them in a room by himself, counting the A's in a picture book or pushing the lever on a time-recording device, the other in a room with the examiner answering his questions. When the individual examiner had completed his work, the subject was either dismissed from the building or taken in charge by another teacher, apart from the subjects who had not yet received the individual tests. The reason for these precautions was to obviate the invalidation of the tests by the intercommunication of the subjects. The schedule of activities will make the plan of operation clear.

GROUP TESTS

1. The first part of the A-test: The subject counts the A's on an unillustrated page of printed matter for a certain period of time, in order that his best rate of speed in doing this work may be determined.

2. Tracing and Opposites Test: This should be given only as a group test. When given singly, the subject's temptation to cheat is inhibited by his fear of being detected.

3. Profile Test. This should be given only as a group test.

4. The first part of the M and N Test: One examiner offers the choice to each member of the group; another examiner records it. This method of procedure saves time; and because of the incident confusion and the division of labor between two examiners tends to obviate the suspicion, when comparisons are made after the tests are over, that the examiners purposely made a mistake.

5. The first part of the Let-Me-Help-You Test: Only one examiner is present to distribute the proper puzzles. This makes it possible for the other examiners to offer help when later they give their subjects the individual tests.

INDIVIDUAL TESTS BY CHIEF EXAMINER
1. Purchasing errand.
2. Borrowing errand.
3. Tip.

INDIVIDUAL TESTS BY ASSISTANT EXAMINER

1. Overstatement Test.
2. The last part of the M and N Test.
3. The last part of the A-Test. The subject counts the A's in a beautifully illustrated book, in order that his rate of speed under this distraction may be compared with the rate when there was no distraction.
4. Pushing-the-Button Test.
5. Let-Me-Help-You Test. This is combined with a test of the subject's ability to solve the Gilbert Wire Puzzles.

The Validity of the Tests

The standardization of mental tests being recognized as a long and difficult process, one of the first questions in connection with this experiment will be whether these tests are valid. A common-sense view would be that they are valid, because they are merely a record of actual responses to actual situations. But immediately the question arises, can one response measure the strength of the particular virtue which is involved? Is it not possible that an individual may respond in a certain way to-day, and in the face of the same situation to-morrow make the very opposite response?

A reasonable reply to this question is that little time was given for making studied responses. The subjects reacted as they probably would react to similar situations if they were made on the spur of the moment. Since ten reactions were secured from each subject in each series of the tests, the chances are that the responses which are better than normal would balance those which are under normal. However, it is undoubtedly true that when a large number of reactions are taken in the testing of any one trait, it is possible to secure a finer measurement than when only one reaction is taken. The Overstatement Test of Series II is an attempt to secure a rather accurate measurement by calling for a number of responses to the same situation.

Perhaps the best evidence of the validity of the tests is a comparison of the results secured by means of them with the opinions of the teachers and Scout leaders who are personally acquainted with the subjects. An inspection of the tabulations will show a rather high correlation between the results of the tests and the opinions of the teachers. In almost every instance where the correlation is low, it happens that the teacher or leader has had but little contact with the members of the group. In those instances where the correlation is very high, the opposite is true: the teacher or leader has had long and intimate acquaintance with the members of the group. The following tabulations of the correlations speak for themselves. In Table I, r stands for the coefficient of correlation (found by the Pearson formula), *Acquaintance* stands for the length of time the teacher or leader has been in contact with the members of the group, and *Number* stands for the number of individual teachers or leaders whose judgment was secured.

TABLE I

CORRELATION OF THE RESULTS OF THE TESTS WITH THE JUDGMENTS OF TEACHERS AND SCOUT LEADERS

Group	r	Acquaintance	Number
A	.928	7 months	4*
B	.410	1 month	1
C	.405	1 month	1
D	.608	6 months	1
E	.299	7 months	3†
F	.753	4 months	1
G	.756	7 months	4*
H	.610	24 months	1
I	.602	2 months	1

* The four judges were the club leader and three teachers. The judgment of the club leader was weighted 2, and the judgments of each of the teachers was weighted 1. Each judgment was secured independently of the others.

† The three judges were three teachers. Their judgment was made jointly and not independently.

INTERCORRELATIONS BETWEEN THE JUDGMENTS OF THE JUDGES

There were four judges for Group A and the same four judges for Group G. The intercorrelations between their judgments are shown in Tables II and III.

TABLE II
Intercorrelations Between the Four Independent Judgments of Group A

\multicolumn{4}{c}{Ranks Given by the Judges}	Correlations
Judge L	Judge K	Judge M	Judge P	
2	1			
6	5			
5	3			$r = .66$
1	2			
4	6			
3	4			
3		1.		
7		4.5		
6		3.5		$r = .46$
2		3.5		
5		7		
4		4.5		
1		2		
3			2.5	
7			6	
6			2.5	
2			1	$r = .48$
5			7	
4			5	
1			4	
	1	1.		
	5	4.5		
	3	2.5		$r = .97$
	2	2.5		
	6	6		
	4	4.5		
	1		2.5	
	5		5	
	3		2.5	$r = .89$
	2		1	
	6		6	
	4		4	
		1	2.5	
		4.5	6	
		3.5	2.5	
		3.5	1	$r = .68$
		7	7	
		4.5	5	
		2	4	

TABLE III

INTERCORRELATIONS BETWEEN THE FOUR INDEPENDENT JUDGMENTS OF GROUP G

Ranks Given by the Judges				Correlations
Judge L	Judge K	Judge M	Judge P	
5	2.5			
6	2.5			
3	1			$r = -.32$
2	4.5			
1	4.5			
4	6			
5		3		
6		3		
3		1		$r = -.03$
2		3		
1		4		
4		5		
6			4.5	
7			3	
4			1	
3			4.5	$r = .22$
1.5			3	
5			7	
1.5			3	
	2.5	3		
	2.5	3		
	1	1		$r = .91$
	4.5	3		
	4.5	5		
	6	6		
	2.5		4.5	
	2.5		2.5	
	1		1	$r = .75$
	4.5		2.5	
	4.5		4.5	
	6		6	
		3	4.5	
		3	2.5	
		1	1	$r = .91$
		3	2.5	
		5	4.5	
		6	6	

These intercorrelations may be summed up in the following tabulation:

Group A

Judges	Correlation
L and K	.66
L and M	.46
L and P	.48
K and M	.97
K and P	.89
M and P	.68

Group G

Judges	Correlation
L and K	—.32
L and M	—.03
L and P	.22
K and M	.91
K and P	.75
M and P	.91

Adding the twelve intercorrelations given in Tables II and III and dividing the sum by 12, we have .55, the correlation of the judgment of one judge with one judge. To find the correlation of the judgment of four judges with four judges, the following formula, taken from Brown's *Mental Measurement*, page 102, was found useful:

$$r_n = \frac{nr_1}{1 + (n-1)r_1}$$

Solving by substituting $r_1 = .55$, and $n = 4$, we find that r_4, the "reliability coefficient," as it has been called by Spearman, is .830.

The question at stake is: Do the objective tests give the whole truth? They probably do not. The only way to arrive at the whole truth would be by means of an infinite number of judgments. However, it is possible to approximate the truth by correcting for the "attenuation" of the coefficients of correlation in Table I because of the chance errors in the obtained data. These chance errors would eliminate themselves if the number of judgments were sufficiently large. By means of Spearman's simplified formula it is possible to correct the correlation coefficients for the attenuation due to chance inaccuracies in the original paired measures, and to ascertain what the true relation would be if an infinite number of judges were to judge an infinite number of these tests; and what the true relation would be if an infinite number of judges were to judge one of the tests. Following is the formula:

$$r_{pq} = \frac{r_{xy}}{\sqrt{r_{x_1x_2} \times r_{y_1y_2}}}$$

If each group had had an equal number of judges, and if each judge had had an *equal acquaintance* with each individual in each group, the problem of correcting for attenuation would be relatively simple. Since this is not the case, correction for attenuation has been attempted by means of the following four solutions:

SOLUTION 1

$$r_{pq} = \frac{r\left(\frac{\text{Groups A and G}}{2}\right)}{\sqrt{r_n \times r_{series\ 1 - series\ 2}}} = \frac{.842}{\sqrt{.83 \times .75}} = \frac{.842}{.78} = 1.06$$

The numerator in the fraction (.842) is obtained by adding the r for Group A, which is .923, to the r for Group G, which is .756, and dividing the result by two. The first factor in the denominator is the reliability coefficient. The second factor in the denominator is the average of the coefficients of correlation between the grades earned by the members of Groups E and I in the first series of tests with the grades earned by the same individuals in the second series of tests. (.63 + .85 = 1.48). Dividing by 2, we have approximately .75. (See Tables I and XXII.)

Solution 2

$$r_{pq} = \frac{r\left(\dfrac{\text{Groups D, H, and I}}{3}\right)}{\sqrt{r_1} \times r_{\text{series 1—series 2}}} = \frac{.607}{\sqrt{.55 \times .75}} = \frac{.607}{.64} = .95$$

The numerator of the fraction (.607) is obtained by adding the r's for Groups D, H, and I (.608, .610 and .602 respectively) and dividing by three. The first factor in the denominator is obtained by adding the twelve intercorrelations given in Tables I and II and dividing the sum by 12. ($r = .55$). The second factor in the denominator is the correlation between the first and second series of tests.

Solution 3

$$r_{pq} = \frac{\dfrac{nr_1}{1+(n-1)r_1}}{\sqrt{r_{\text{Group E}}} \times r_{\text{series 1—series 2}}} = \frac{.46}{\sqrt{.299 \times .75}} = \frac{.46}{.47} = .97$$

The numerator of the fraction is the reliability coefficient that is obtained from the correlation of the results of the tests with the judgments of the teachers, who judged Group E. Since their judgment was a joint judgment, it was assumed that three joint judgments would equal two independent judgments, and "2" was substituted for n in the formula for finding r_n. The first factor in the denominator is the r between the findings of the tests and the judgments of the judges of Group E; the second factor in the denominator is the correlation between the first and the second series of tests.

Solution 4

$$r_{pq} = \frac{r\left(\dfrac{\text{Groups B and C}}{2}\right)}{\sqrt{r_{\text{assumed}}} \times r_{\text{series 1—series 2}}} = \frac{.408}{\sqrt{.40 \times .75}} = \frac{.408}{\sqrt{.3}} = .75$$

The numerator of the fraction is obtained by adding the *r*'s for Groups B and C and dividing by 2. (See Table I.) The first factor in the denominator is assumed. If the correlation is .55 with seven months' acquaintance, the assumption is that it would be approximately .40 with one month's acquaintance. The second factor in the denominator is the correlation between the first and the second series of tests.

The data in Table I, therefore, having been corrected for attenuation, may be interpreted to mean that the actual agreement between the judgments of an infinite number of judges with an infinite number of these tests would not be less than .75.

In order to find the actual agreement between the judgments of an infinite number of judges with *one* of these tests, it is only necessary to substitute 1.00, a perfect correlation, for .75, the actual correlation between the tests of Series 1 and Series 2, in the formulae used in the four solutions given above. The results are as follows:

$$\text{Solution 1} = \frac{.842}{\sqrt{.83 \times 1}} = \frac{.842}{.911} = .924$$

$$\text{Solution 2} = \frac{.607}{\sqrt{.55 \times 1}} = \frac{.607}{.741} = .805$$

$$\text{Solution 3} = \frac{.46}{\sqrt{.29 \times 1}} = \frac{.46}{.55} = .83$$

$$\text{Solution 4} = \frac{.408}{\sqrt{.40 \times 1}} = \frac{.408}{.632} = .646$$

No allowance has been made as yet for the difference in the values of the judgments based upon different lengths of acquaintance. The weighting scheme on page 90 will show that when such allowance is made, the correlations increase with the weightings.

It thus appears that the average correlation of .80 is increased to .87 and .85 respectively when greater importance is attached

Solution	Groups	Months	Judges	r	Weight	Product	
1	2	7	4	.92	1	.92	
2	3	6,24,2	1	.81	1	.81	Av.r
3	1	7	2*	.83	1	.83	=.80
4	2	1	1	.65	1	.65	
1	2	7	4	.92	3	2.76	
2	3	6,24,2	1	.81	2	1.62	Av.r
3	1	7	2*	.83	1	.83	=.87
4	2	1	1	.65	1	.65	
1	2	7	4	.92	5	4.60	
2	3	6,24,2	1	.81	3	2.43	Av.r
3	1	7	2*	.83	2	1.66	=.85
4	2	1	1	.65	1	.65	

*Three judges, not independent, were assumed to be equal to two judges acting independently of each other.

to the length of the acquaintance of the judges with the subjects. The same holds true with regard to the r's obtained from the four solutions for the value of r when an infinite number of judgments are correlated with an infinite number of these tests. In the following tabulation the same weighting scheme is followed as in the table immediately preceding:

Solution	Groups	Months	Judges	r	Weight	Product	
1	2	7	4	1.06	1	1.06	
2	3	6,24,2	1	.95	1	.95	Av.r
3	1	7	2*	.97	1	.97	=.93
4	2	1	1	.75	1	.75	
1	2	7	4	1.06	3	3.18	
2	3	6,24,2	1	.95	2	1.90	Av.r
3	1	7	2*	.97	1	.97	=.97
4	2	1	1	.75	1	.75	
1	2	7	4	1.06	5	5.30	
2	3	6,24,2	1	.95	3	2.85	Av.r
3	1	7	2*	.97	2	1.94	=.99
4	2	1	1	.75	1	.75	

*Three judges, not independent, were assumed to be equal to two judges acting independently of each other.

From this table it appears that the average correlation of .93 is increased to .97 and .99 respectively when greater importance is attached to the length of the acquaintance of the judges with the subjects.

CAN THE TESTS BE ECONOMIZED?

Since there is considerable labor attached to giving a series of ten tests, one important question that presents itself is, Will it be possible to arrive at the same results by the use of only a few tests?

In order to ascertain the relative value of the different tests of Series I the following method was followed:

By trial the three best tests were selected. They were tests 5, 9 and 10. Their scores were then combined by adding and the sums were correlated with the criterion of each group. The next step was to correlate the results of tests 5, 9 and 10 with the rank obtained in the total series. The next step was to correlate tests 5, 9 and 10 with tests 1, 2, and 3. Tests 1, 2, and 3 were then correlated with the criteria, and finally tests 1, 2 and 3 were correlated with the total scores. Table IV (page 92) gives the correlations and the averages.

The results show that the average correlation between the rank obtained by the test and the rank given by the teacher was almost .60; that the average correlation between the best tests and the criterion was .44; that the average correlation between the best tests and the rank obtained in the total series was .74; that the average correlation between the best tests and the first three tests was .28; that the average correlation between the first three tests and the criterion was .32; and that the average correlation between the first three tests and the total scores was .48. In other words, if the three best tests alone were used the results would be only about 70 per cent as satisfactory as those obtained by the use of all of the tests; also the correlation between the best three tests and three others chosen indiscriminately is very low. The conclusion is that the tests of the first series cannot be any further economized.

No effort was made to evaluate the separate tests of Series II. However, a comparison of the results will show that Test 1 of Series II shows a very high degree of correlation with the total results of the series. Teachers desiring to give an easy test of trustworthiness can get approximate results by using Test 1 of Series II.

TABLE IV

1. Original r, between rank obtained by test and criterion (rank given by teacher).
2. Between Tests 5, 9, and 10 of Series I (which by process of trial and error have been found to be the best three of the series) and the criterion.
3. Between Tests 5, 9, and 10 of Series I and the rank obtained in the total series.
4. Between Tests 5, 9, and 10, and Tests 1, 2, and 3.
5. Between Tests 1, 2, and 3 and the criterion.
6. Between 1, 2, and 3 with the total scores.

Group	1	2	3	4	5	6
A	.92	.77	.88	.19	0	.19
B	.41	.34	.58	—.17	0	.45
C	.40	.31	.65	.31	—.16	.61
D	.60	.31	.72	.48	.37	.55
E	.29	.44	.87	.06	.31	.25
F	.75	.38	.59	.48	.43	.38
G	.75	.55	.83	.55	.77	.83
H	.61	.28	.81	.45	.65	.60
I	.60	.61	.78	.22	.56	.50
Average Correlations	.59	.44	.74	.28	.32	.48

THE RESULTS OF THE FIRST SERIES OF TESTS

It will be noted that in summing up the separate grades earned by each subject to get his total score, the same importance was attached to all features of the series. It is possible that a fairer and more accurate way would be to give double weight to Tests 5, 9, and 10, which are designed to measure the subject's honesty. However, trustworthiness is something more than honesty. A subject who is too easily swayed by suggestion, who is easily distracted from his task by accidental circumstances, or who forgets to keep his promises, may be honest and not trustworthy. For this reason the same values were attached to the results of each of the tests. The measure employed is doubtless crude, but it is the best that could be secured with the limited means at the disposal of the investigator.

The results of the first series of tests are given in Tables V to XVI inclusive. Following is the key to the contents of all the tables of Series I.

Ind. = Individual. The name is omitted for obvious reasons.
Age. = Age in years.
  1 = Assenting to overstatement regarding his grades.
  2 = Yielding to the suggestion that he made a mistake.
  3 = Accepting help contrary to his instructions.
  4 = Returning or delivering articles according to promise.
  5 = Keeping ten cents overchange.
  6 = Accepting ten cent tip for small favor.
  7 = Pushing a button according to instructions.
  8 = Counting A s in a picture book as rapidly as in an uninteresting book.
  9 = Peeping at a profile when on honor to keep his eyes closed.
  10 = Cheating by adding words after test was over.
  M = Merits and demerits. Merits are indicated by the plus sign; demerits by the minus sign.
  G = Grade. This is obtained by adding the scores and the merits and demerits.
  R = Rank given by the tests.
  RL = Rank given by the judgment of the teacher or leader.
  IQ = Intelligence Quotient.

TABLE V

Series I. Group A

Ind.	Age	1	2	3	4	5	6	7	8	9	10	M	G	R	RL	IQ
1	10	10	2	10	0	10	10	5	10	10	10		77	3	2	148
2*	10	0	3	10	10	0	0	2	7	0	0	—10	22	7	7	133
3	11	0	4	5	10	0	0	2	10	7	0		38	6	5	142
4	11	2	10	10	0	10	10	10	10	10	10		82	2	3	151
5†	13	10	9	10	10	10	0	6	7	0	0	—20	42	5	6	135
6††	10	10	10	10	10	0	10	8	10	0	10	—10	68	4	4	146
7	11	10	3	10	10	10	10	10	10	10	5		88	1	1	139

*Removed money from a pocket book which he found and then returned the book to the Lost and Found Department.

†Told a falsehood on his own initiative; stopped in the midst of an assigned task to attend to other matters of interest to him.

††Stopped in the midst of an assigned task to attend to other matters of interest to him.

Correlation between the ranks obtained by the tests and those given by the four teachers = .928.

TABLE VI

Series I. Group B

Ind.	Age	1	2	3	4	5	6	7	8	9	10	M	G	R	RL
1	12	0	10	0	10	10	10	2	9	7	10		68	3	4
2	13	0	10	10	10	10	10	6	10	0	0		66	4	1
3	13	0	10	0	10	10	10	4	10	0	10		64	5	7
4	13	10	10	10	0	10	0	10	9	10	10		79	1	9
5	14	10	10	0	0	10	10	6	10	0	0		56	8.5	10
6	13	0	10	10	10	10	0	10	10	0	0		60	6	8
7	13	0	8	0	0	10	10	10	9	0	10		57	7	6
8	15	0	9	10	0	10	0	10	8	5	0		52	10	2
9	13	10	3	0	0	10	10	8	10	0	0		51	11	12
10	13	0	10	10	0	10	10	10	10	7	10		77	2	3
11	13	10	2	0	0	10	10	5	6	3	10		56	8.5	5
12	14	0	4	0	0	10	0	6	10	0	10		40	12	11

$r = .41$

TABLE VII

Series I. Group C

Ind.	Age	1	2	3	4	5	6	7	8	9	10	M	G	R	RL
1		0	10	0	0	0	0	0	10	3	0		23	11	8
2		10	6	10	10	10	0	10	10	10	0		76	2	5
3	15	0	2	10	10	10	0	0	10	3	10		55	8	3
4*	13	10	10	0	0	10	0	6	10	0	0	—10	36	9	10
5	16	0	10	10	0	10	10	4	10	3	10		67	5	2
6	17	0	8	10	10	10	10	10	9	7	10		84	1	1
7	14	10	10	10	0	10	0	8	7	7	0		62	6	9
8†	16	0	10	5	0	10	0	6	10	10	10	— 5	56	7	11
9		10	10	10	0	10	0	2	10	10	10		72	4	6
10	14	0	10	0	0	10	0	4	10	0	0		34	10	7
11	15	0	10	10	10	10	0	8	10	7	10		75	3	4

*Told a falsehood on his own initiative.
†Absent without making excuse.

$r = .405$

See page 93 for key to captions.

TABLE VIII

Series I. Group D

Ind.	Age	1	2	3	4	5	6	7	8	9	10	M	G	R	RL
1	12	10	10	0	0	10	10	4	10	10	10		74	10	11
2	16	10	10	10	10	10	10	10	10	7	10		97	1	3
3	14	10	10	0	10	10	10	8	10	7	0		75	9	5
4	16	10	10	0	10	10	10	8	10	10	0		78	8	6
5	13	10	6	7	10	10	10	10	10	3	10		86	4	8
6	15	10	10	8	10	0	10	6	10	7	0		71	11	4
7	14	10	10	10	10	10	10	6	10	10	10		96	2	1
8	13	10	10	10	0	10	10	8	10	10	10		88	3	2
9	14	10	10	0	0	0	10	10	10	3	0		53	12	12
10	13	10	10	10	0	10	10	2	10	10	10		82	6	9
11	16	10	10	10	0	10	10	10	10	10	0		80	7	10
12	14	10	8	0	10	10	10	10	10	7	10		85	5	7

$r = .608$

TABLE IX

Series I. Group E

Ind.	Age	1	2	3	4	5	6	7	8	9	10	M	G	R	RL
1	13	0	10	10	0	10	10	8	10	7	0		65	12	8
2	13	5	10	10	0	0	0	8	10	0	0		43	14	14
3	12	10	0	10	10	10	10	0	10	10	10		80	4.5	11
4	13	10	10	10	0	10	0	10	10	7	0		67	10.5	1
5	14	10	10	10	0	0	10	10	10	7	10		77	8	12
6	13	10	10	0	0	10	10	10	10	7	0		67	10.5	5
7	13	0	10	10	10	10	10	8	10	10	0		78	7	6
8	14	10	10	10	10	10	10	10	10	10	10		100	1	2
9	12	0	10	10	10	10	10	8	10	10	10		88	2.5	7
10	10	5	10	0	0	10	10	10	10	10	10		75	9	4
11	15	0	10	0	10	10	10	6	10	7	0		63	13	9
12	12	10	10	10	0	10	10	8	10	10	10		88	2.5	3
13*	12	0	10	10	10	10	10	8	10	10	0	+1	79	6	13
14	17	0	10	10	10	10	10	10	10	10	0		80	4.5	10

*Called attention to his having missed pushing the button.

$r = .299$

See page 93 for key to captions.

TABLE X

Series I. Group F

Ind.	Age	1	2	3	4	5	6	7	8	9	10	M	G	R	RL
1	12	10	10	0	10	10	10	5	10	3	0		68	3	3
2	12	10	10	0	0	10	0	8	10	7	0		55	8	8
3	12	10	10	0	0	10	10	4	10	3	0		57	6.5	4
4*	12	10	10	0	10	0	10	10	10	0	0	—10	50	9	9
5	14	10	10	0	10	10	10	6	10	7	10		83	1	2
6	11	10	10	0	0	10	10	6	10	3	10		69	2	5
7	13	10	10	0	10	0	10	5	10	3	0		58	5	7
8	13	10	10	0	10	10	0	4	10	3	0		57	6.5	6
9	13	10	10	0	10	0	10	10	10	3	0		63	4	1

*Told falsehood about not knowing she had money in her pocket.

$r = .753$

TABLE XI

Series I. Group G

Ind.	Age	1	2	3	4	5	6	7	8	9	10	M	G	R	RL
1	10	10	10	10	0	10	10	10	10	7	10		87	3	1.5
2	13	5	10	9	0	10	10	10	10	7	0		71	5	7
3	10	10	10	10	0	10	10	10	10	10	10		90	2	4
4	10	5	10	10	0	10	10	10	10	0	0		65	6	5
5	12	10	10	0	0	10	0	6	10	5	0		51	7	6
6	11	10	9	10	10	10	10	9	10	10	10		98	1	1.5
7	13	10	8	10	0	10	10	8	10	10	10		86	4	3

$r = .756$

See page 93 for key to captions.

TABLE XII

Series I. Group H

Ind.	Age	1	2	3	4	5	6	7	8	9	10	M	G	R	RL
1	15	10	10	10	10	10	10	5	10	10	10		95	2	10
2	17	10	10	10	0	10	10	8	10	5	0		73	11	5
3	16	5	10	10	0	0	10	9	10	3	0		57	12	11
4*	15	10	10	10	0	10	10	5	10	10	10	—5	80	8	8.5
5	13	10	10	10	0	0	10	10	10	10	10		80	8	8.5
6	17	10	10	10	0	10	10	10	9	3	10		82	6	2
7	15	10	10	10	0	10	10	10	10	10	10		90	3	1
8	16	10	10	10	0	10	10	6	10	10	10		86	5	4
9	16	10	10	10	0	10	10	7	10	3	10		80	8	7
10	15	10	10	10	10	10	10	7	10	10	10		97	1	3
11	14	5	10	10	10	10	10	5	5	4	10		79	10	12
12	18	10	10	10	0	10	10	9	10	10	10		89	4	6

*Demerit for using profane language during test. His leader had frequently warned him against doing this.

$r = .61$

TABLE XIII

Series I. Group I

Ind.	Age	1	2	3	4	5	6	7	8	9	10	M	G	R	RL	IQ
1	12	10	10	10	0	10	0	3	10	0	0		53	3	6	109
2	12	10	8	0	0	10	0	7	10	3	0		48	5	7	97
3	11	10	2	0	0	10	0	7	10	3	10		52	4	4	141
4	11	10	10	0	0	10	0	2	9	0	0		41	7	5	100
5	11	10	7	10	0	10	0	0	10	0	0		47	6	3	100
6*	12	10	10	0	0	10	0	3	10	0	0	—10	33	8	8	115
7	12	10	10	10	5	10	10	10	10	10	10		95	1	2	61
8	11	10	10	10	10	10	0	6	10	10	10		86	2	1	101

*Found a purse and kept it without attempting to find owner.

$r = .602$

See page 93 for key to captions.

TABLE XIV

Series I. Group J

Ind.	Age	1	2	3	4	5	6	7	8	9	10	M	G	R
1	12	0	10	0	0	0	0	0	10	3	0		23	10
2	13	0	10	0	0	0	0	2	5	7	0		24	9
3	12	0	10	0	10	10	0	10	10	7	0		57	3
4	12	0	10	0	0	0	0	6	10	10	0		36	7.5
5	13	0	10	0	0	0	0	10	10	5	10		45	5
6	12	0	10	0	0	10	0	6	10	0	0		36	7.5
7	12	0	10	0	10	10	0	6	10	10	10		66	2
8	12	0	10	0	0	10	10	3	10	3	0		46	4
9	12	10	10	10	0	10	0	10	10	10	0		70	1
10	13	0	10	0	10	0	0	5	10	3	0		38	6
11	12	0	0	0	0	10	0	2	10	0	0		22	11

Average = 42

TABLE XV

Series I. Group K

Ind.	Age	1	2	3	4	5	6	7	8	9	10	M	G	R
1	13	2	3	0	10	10	0	10	10	3	0		48	10
2	12	4	10	0	10	10	0	5	10	0	0		49	8
3	14	2	10	0	10	0	0	0	10	0	0		42	12
4	13	4	10	10	0	10	0	5	10	10	0		59	3
5	13	8	10	10	10	10	0	2	10	10	10		80	1
6	14	8	10	0	10	0	0	2	10	10	0		50	6
7	12	4	10	0	0	10	10	4	10	10	0		58	4
8	13	0	10	0	10	10	0	10	10	10	0		60	2
9	12	6	3	10	10	0	0	2	9	3	0		43	11
10	13	3	10	0	10	10	0	10	8	3	0		54	5
11	14	8	10	0	10	0	0	5	9	7	0		49	8
12	14	0	8	0	10	10	0	8	10	3	0		49	8

Average = 53.4

See page 93 for key to captions.

TABLE XVI

Summary of the Results of the First Series of Tests

Group	Character	Amount of Training	Average in Test	Rank
A	Private School	None	59.5	7
B	Boy Scouts	Just organized	60.5	6
C	Boy Scouts	Just organized	58.1	8
D	Boy Scouts	Six months	80.4	2
E	Private School	None	75.0	4
F	Camp Fire Girls	Four months	62.2	5
G	Private School	None	78.2	3
H	Boy Scouts	Two years	82.3	1
I	Public School	None	56.8	9
J	Boy Scouts	Just organized	42.1	11
K	Boy Scouts	Just organized	53.4	10

It will be noted that Group H, which averaged the highest in the tests, is a Boy Scout troop which had been in training for a period of two years. The leader of this troop is the same man who is in charge of Group C, which is one of the experimental groups, and which had just been organized when these tests were made. Group D, which ranks second in these tests, had been in training under a good Boy Scout leader for a period of six months. Groups G and E, which rank respectively third and fourth in the tests, seem to be made up of boys who come from rather good homes. Group J, which ranks lowest in the tests, is made up of boys who do not seem to have the advantages of good home training, and whose public school training is not designed to improve them in trustworthiness.

The Two Series of Tests Compared

The two experimental groups were Groups B and C. The two control groups were Groups E and I. The groups were well chosen, with the exception of Group E, which seems to be made up of individuals having an environment quite superior to that of the other groups. Every precaution was taken to give like treatment to the two experimental groups, and to avoid giving any special training to the two control groups. The Boy Scout leaders were ignorant of the nature of the tests and hence could not have given any special coaching in anticipation of them, even if they had purposed to do so.

The two series of tests are as nearly alike in character as it was possible to make them without revealing to the subjects the nature of the tests, and without invalidating the results of the second series through the practice effect of the first. During both series of tests no mention was made to the subjects of the nature of the tests, or of the words "morality" or "trustworthiness," although the examiners were frequently questioned by the subjects on this matter. One of the little New York boys guessed that they were tests of "noive," (meaning "nerve"). The subjects were given to understand that the tests were "mental" tests, and it is not believed that any but the brightest ones discovered their specific character.

While the character of the two tests is as nearly on a par as it was possible to make them, the second series is more severe than the first. Several prizes are offered during the progress of the second test, and the attractiveness of these prizes, added to the desire to stand well in the tests, should create rather powerful motives to yield to the temptations which are offered in the tests.

The first test in the second series is perhaps a more accurate measure of a subject's tendency to make overstatements than the first test of Series I. The second test of Series II is something more than a test of suggestibility, while the second test of Series I is nothing more. The third test of the second series is a trifle different from the third test of the first series, in that the latter offers the temptation by means of a person, while the former simply gives the subject the opportunity to help himself. The fifth test of the second series, which offers the subject the temptation to keep twenty-five cents which do not belong to him, is a stronger temptation than to keep only ten cents, which is the opportunity offered in the fifth test of the first series. It is believed that all the other tests of Series II are on a par with the corresponding tests of Series I.

Series II of the Tests

1. The Overstatement Test

Can the subject be trusted to make true statements in regard to his knowledge?

DIRECTIONS: Give each subject the following blank, instructing him to write a grade of 10 whenever his answer is in the affirmative, and a grade of 0 when his answer is in the negative. Instruct him also to add the grades to obtain the score.

No. 1

Grades

1. Can you swim?..
2. Can you skate on ice skates? ....
3. Can you skate on roller skates?.............................
4. Can you drive a car?...
5. Can you ride on horse back?.................................
6. Can you row a boat?..
7. Can you walk on stilts?......................................
8. Can you operate a typewriter?...............................
9. Can you operate an adding machine?..........................
10. Can you run an elevator?....................................
    Score....................

The individual who reports the highest score is awarded a prize. The purpose of this questionnaire and of the prize is to create a motive for making overstatements on the blank which follows.

No. 2

(Grading and Scoring the same as in No. 1)   *Grades*

1. Do you know all the letters of the alphabet in their order?......
2. Do you know how to write any number up to ten million?......
3. Do you know all of the multiplication tables up to the tens?..
4. Do you know the name of the capital of each state of the union?...
5. Do you know the names of all of the Presidents of the United States from Washington to Wilson?.................
6. Do you know the names of all of the oceans and the continents?..
7. Do you know how to write decimals?........................

8. Do you know who invented the steamboat, the cotton gin, the electric light, and the wireless telegraph?......
9. Do you know how many inches in a foot, how many feet in a yard, how many yards in a rod, and how many feet in a mile?.....................................
10. Do you know how to add fractions?........................
Score ....

When the scores are announced, the one reporting the highest score is again awarded a prize. In case of tie, the prize is drawn by lot.

SCORING: To obtain a score in this test, the replies are compared with the replies received from the following questions given in the Quiz Test:

2. How much is 8 times 9?
3. How many yards in a rod?
4. Write six hundred seventy thousand forty five, and eight thousandths.
5. Who invented the wireless telegraph?
6. Add one-half and one-fifth.
7. What is the seventh letter of the alphabet?
8. Name all of the oceans.
9. Name the third President of the United States.

(Questions 1 and 10 of the Quiz Test are not considered because they are not pertinent to this test.)

Correct replies to each of the questions in the Quiz Test list are valued at 1, except the reply to question 4, which, when correct, is given a value of 3 points. After these values have been added, each subject is given an additional credit of 1 point on each point of failure in the Quiz Test, *provided* his reply to the corresponding question in No. 2 was zero. The sum of the values plus the sum of the credits is the score.

2. TEST OF TRUTHFULNESS AND SUGGESTIBILITY

Can the subject be trusted not to yield readily to suggestion on matters of fact when the facts are at hand, and can he be trusted to tell the truth regarding himself even at the expense of his pride?

DIRECTIONS: Give each subject the following set of questions, instructing him to write a grade of from 0 to 10 in reply to each question.

No. 3

Grades
1. About what grade should be given to you in school or scout spirit? ....
2. In conduct? ....
3. In industry? ....
4. In reliability? ....
5. In obedience to your parents? ....
6. In good manners? ....
7. In truthfulness? ....
8. In honesty? ....
9. In courage? ....
10. In willingness to help others? ....

Score ....

The subject is then given another copy of the same blank and instructed to make a duplicate. The examiner collects the originals and requests each subject to put his duplicate into his pocket.

Interval (during which the examiner's assistant takes the originals into another room in order to refer to them while filling in part of question 4 of No. 4.)

No. 4 is then submitted to the subject. Question 4 being the only one pertinent to this test, the others are here omitted.

Question 4: *Why did you give yourself the following grades?*

Two grades are mentioned, one being higher than the subject gave himself and one being lower. It will be recalled that each subject has in his pocket a copy of the grades which he actually gave himself, so that it is possible for him to verify the grades mentioned on the blank if he wishes to do so.

SCORING: The first half of this test counts 5 points, and the second half counts 5 points.

Add the grades which the subject has given himself in reliability, truthfulness, and honesty. Take the sum of these as the numerator of a fraction, the denominator of which is 30, then take the sum of the grades which the subject earns in the second half of this test plus his grade in Test 9 plus his grade in Test 10 (counting 10 as a perfect record in each), and use this sum as the numerator of another fraction the denominator of which is also 30. Invert the first fraction, multiply it by the second fraction, and divide the result by 2 to obtain the score for the first half of the test.

The score for the second half of this test is 5 if the subject calls attention to the discrepancy in the grades. It is 0 if he fails to do so.

Add the results of the first and second halves to obtain the score for the entire test.

3. RECEIVING-HELP TEST

Can the subject be trusted to work independently when he has been instructed to do so?

DIRECTIONS: The subject is handed the Quiz Test, which is typed on a four-page folder with the questions on page 1 and the answers on page 4. Care is taken to place the folder on the subject's desk with the first page up. The subject is instructed NOT to look on page 4 of the folder. He is not told that the answers are on page 4, but he is led to infer that they are, because of the fact that in the Completion Test, which is given immediately before the Quiz Test, he was required to look on page 4 when correcting his replies.

(These tests are described in a different order from which they are given, simply to facilitate comparisons between the results obtained in the first and second series of tests. The correct order of giving them will be mentioned under the caption "The Administration of the Tests of Series II.")

During part of the Quiz Test the examiner leaves the room so that the subject may have opportunity to look on the forbidden page 4 if he chooses to do so. Some of the answers given on page 4 are of course incorrect.

Following is the Quiz Test. It will be recalled that some of the questions were quoted in the description of the Overstatement Test.

QUIZ TEST. (Page 1)

1. Which is correct, "6 and 7 *are* 14" or "6 and 7 *is* 14"?......
2. How much is 8 times 9?...
3. How many yards in a rod?..
4. Write six hundred seventy three thousand forty five and eight thousandths.................................
5. Who invented the wireless telegraph?............................
6. Add one-half and one-fifth..
7. What is the seventh letter of the alphabet?.....................

8. Name all the oceans..
   ....
9. Name the third President of the United States...............
10. How do you make 100 out of four nines?....................

Quiz Test. (Page 4)

1. 6 and 7 are 13.
2. 74.
3. 6 and one-half.
4. 673,045.0008.
5. Edison.
6. 8/10.
7. g.
8. Arctic, Antarctic, Atlantic, Pacific, South Sea and Indian.
9. Adams.
10. 99 and 9/9.

SCORING: Score the subject 10 if there is no evidence that he has copied any answers from page 4. Score him 0 if there is evidence that he has copied.

4. RELIABILITY TEST

Can the subject be trusted to deliver a letter and to see that a reply is mailed within twenty-four hours if he promises to do so? Can he be trusted not to read the letter if the envelope is left unsealed?

DIRECTIONS: Hand the subject a large envelope containing (a) a very small envelope with a dime enclosed, (b) Blank No. 4 which is reproduced below, and (c) an envelope (unsealed) containing the examiner's self-addressed stamped envelope and a letter addressed to the subject's parent, teacher, or guardian.

The subject is requested to open the large envelope, to read and fill out Blank No. 4 and to return the same to the examiner.

The purpose of questions 2 and 3 is to commit the subject to a definite promise. The purpose of question 4 has been stated in the description of the Test of Truthfulness and Suggestibility. The purpose of the dime will be revealed in the description of the sixth test.

Blank No. 4 reads as follows:

No. 4

Please fill out this blank and put it back into the large envelope. Do not let anyone know what answers you write.

1. Your name..
2. Will you hand the enclosed letter to your father, mother, guardian or teacher, and see that an answer is mailed to me within 24 hours?..
3. Will you agree not to read the letter which I am sending, nor to read the answer?....................................
4. Why did you give yourself the following grades?............
....
....

Thank you for answering these questions. In the very small envelope enclosed herewith is a dime, which I will ask you to accept for your trouble.

The letter to the parent, guardian or teacher reads as follows:

TO THE PARENT, GUARDIAN, OR TEACHER:

I am making a study of boys. Will you help me by answering the following questions in regard to..
Please do not let him know what answers you write. A prompt reply will be appreciated. Please use the enclosed stamped envelope for your reply.

1. Does he take an interest in school or scout work?............
2. Is he good in his conduct?..................................
3. Is he industrious?..
4. Is he reliable?...
5. Does he obey his teachers and parents?.....................
6. Does he use good manners?..................................
7. Is he truthful?..
8. Is he honest?..
9. Is he courageous?..
10. Is he willing to help others?..............................

Thanking you for your help, I am
Yours sincerely
(Examiner's name.)

Please sign your name on the line below.

_____

SCORING: Score the subject 10 if a reply is received from parent, guardian or teacher within five days. Score him 0 if no reply is received, or if there is conclusive evidence, either that he has written and signed the letter himself or that he has influenced the answer.

5. Honesty Test

Can the subject be trusted not to keep 25 cents which have been mailed to him by "mistake"?

DIRECTIONS: On the stationery of some well-known business house, mail to each subject the following letter, with a twenty-five cent piece enclosed in a coin card.

DEAR FRIEND:

Enclosed find twenty-five cents to balance our account to date. You will be glad to learn that our Boys' Advertising Campaign was a success. Please sign the receipt at the foot of this page and return to us in the enclosed stamped envelope at your early convenience.

Thanking you for your help, and hoping to have your co-operation at some future time, we are,

Yours truly,
(Firm's Name)
(Per Advertising Manager)
Place and Date

Received of.................................twenty-five cents to balance account to date.

(Signed)..............................

SCORING: Score the subject 10 if the money is returned. Score him 0 if he fails to return it.

6. The Tip Test

Can the subject be trusted not to accept a tip for a trifling courtesy?

DIRECTIONS: This test is a repetition of the sixth test of Series I, the only difference being that in this instance the tip is given to the subject in a letter, while in the former test it was handed to him personally. The opportunity of offering the subject a tip is furnished in the administration of the Reliability Test.

SCORING: The subject is scored 0 if he accepts the tip; he is scored 10 if he refuses it.

7. The Push Button Test

This test is exactly the same as the seventh test described under Series I.

8. "A" Test

This test is the same as the eighth test described under Series I.

108   *The Function of Ideals and Attitudes in Social Education*

9. The Cardboard Test

Can the subject be trusted not to peep when he is placed on his honor to keep his eyes closed?

DIRECTIONS: The principle and the method in this test are the same as in the Profile Test described under Series 1. The apparatus only is different.

Each subject is handed a card 12 inches by 12 inches. On the card are five circles, each five-eighths of an inch in diameter. The circles are located at the angles of an imaginary equilateral pentagon, the sides of which are six and one half inches long.

Following is a diagram of the arrangement of the circles, the dimensions of the imaginary pentagon being reduced in size.

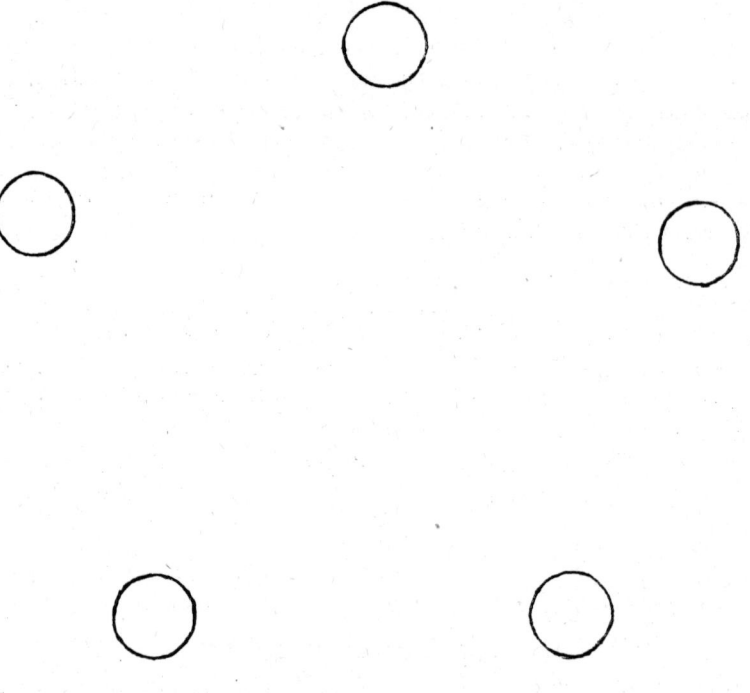

The subject is instructed to look carefully at the circles and then with eyes closed to try to place a pencil mark in each of the five circles as his hand sweeps around the circumference of the pentagon. If he places a mark in each circle as he goes once around, he writes on a card, "First trial, correct"; if he fails, he writes, "First trial, wrong." He is given five trials. The individual reporting the highest number of successes is awarded a prize.

SCORING: A subject who reports one or more successes in the five trials is scored 0. A subject who reports only failures is scored 10. This feat is impossible of accomplishment as far as it has been possible to determine. The examiner himself, after long practice and fifty successive trials, was unable to score a single success. No trustworthy subject has been found who is able to accomplish the feat.

10. COMPLETION TEST

Can the subject be trusted not to cheat in an examination?

This test is given on a prepared four-page folder, the sentences with the blanks being on page one, and the completed sentences being on page four. Page two is entirely blank. Page three has a coating of paraffine. The paraffine coating may be applied by heating a candle and rubbing it on the paper and then scraping off the lumps with a dull knife.

COMPLETION TEST. (Page 1)

Name...
Write only one word on each blank. Time Limit: Six Minutes
1. Boys and..............soon become.............and women.
2. The.............are often more contented..........the rich.
3. The rose is a favorite.............because of..........fragrance and..............
4. It is very..................to become.....................
   acquainted.................persons who.............timid.
5. Extremely old..............sometimes..............almost
   as...............care as..................
6. The stars and the...............will shine tonight.
7. Time.................often more valuable..............money.
8. The poor baby..................as if it were.............sick.
9. She................if she will.
10. Brothers and sisters.............always................. to
    help...............other and should...............quarrel.

COMPLETION TEST. (Page 4)

1. Boys and girls soon become men and women.
2. The poor are often more contented than the rich.

3. The rose is a favorite flower because of its fragrance and beauty.
4. It is very difficult to become well acquainted with persons who are timid.
5. Extremely old people sometimes need almost as much care as infants.
6. The stars and the moon will shine tonight.
7. Time is often more valuable than money.
8. The poor baby acts as if it were very sick.
9. She can if she will.
10. Brothers and sisters should always try to help each other and should not quarrel.

DIRECTIONS: The method of giving this test is as follows: A folder is placed before each subject, face side up. The subject is told that the completed sentences are on page 4 and for that reason he is not to look on page 4. The examiner remains in the room to see that these instructions are obeyed.

When the time is up, the subject is requested to open the folder and to place it on the desk before him in such manner that he can see pages 1 and 4 at the same time. This procedure will lessen the chances of the subject's discovery of the paraffined page on the inside of the folder, which contains a record of his effort to complete the test. The subject is requested to score his own paper, using page 4 as his model. During this part of the work the examiner absents himself to give the subject opportunity to cheat if he desires to do so.

A comparison of the record made on the waxed surface, with the record as handed in on page 1 will reveal whether the subject attempted to cheat.

SCORING: Score the subject 10 if he made no attempt to cheat. Score him 0 if he did.

THE ADMINISTRATION OF THE TESTS OF SERIES II

The tests just described are much easier to administer than the tests of Series I. All but three may be given as group tests. Two examiners can do all of the work. In two hours' time it is possible for two examiners to test twelve or fifteen subjects.

The second series of tests has another advantage over the first series in that each subject makes his own records, the possibility of error on the part of the examiner being thus reduced to a minimum. There is a second advantage possessed by

Series II in that the mass of material which is presented makes it impossible for any subject to remember all the details, in case he should attempt to describe the tests to prospective subjects.

The group tests were given in the following order:
1. Blank No. 1. 2. Blank No. 2.
3. Blank No. 3. 4. Cardboard Test.
5. Marking A's in book containing no illustrations.
6. Blank No. 4. 7. Completion Test. 8. Quiz Test.

The Honesty Test was given by mail. The Time Stamp Test and the second half of the A-Test (counting A's in a beautifully illustrated book) were given individually by either the examiner or his assistant.

If the examiners had had unlimited time at their disposal, a few of the tests given in group would have been given individually. Among these are the Quiz Test, and perhaps also the Cardboard and the Completion Tests. The reason for this is that it is impossible entirely to prevent communication between subjects. A particularly shrewd subject, discovering that some of the answers given on page 4 of the Quiz Test are not correct, can invalidate the test by passing the word during the absence of the examiner from the room.

THE RESULTS OF THE SECOND SERIES OF TESTS

The results are given in Tables XVII to XXII inclusive. Following is the key to the contents of all of the tables of Series II:

Ind. = Individual. The name is omitted for obvious reasons.
Age = Age in years.
 1 = Making an overstatement regarding his knowledge.
 2 = Making and accepting unverified statements.
 3 = Receiving aid during test contrary to instructions.
 4 = Delivering a letter according to promise.
 5 = Keeping 25 cents sent to him by "mistake."
 6 = Accepting ten cent tip for doing a small favor.
 7 = Stamping the time clock according to instructions.
 8 = Counting A's in picture book as fast as in "dry" book.
 9 = Peeping at circles when on honor to keep eyes closed.
 10 = Cheating by adding words to completion test.
 G = Grade. This is obtained by adding the scores.
 R = Rank given by the tests.
 RL = Rank given by the judgment of the teacher or leader.
 IQ = Intelligence quotient.

TABLE XVII

Series II. Group B

Ind.	Age	1	2	3	4	5	6	7	8	9	10	G	R	IQ
1	12	5	8	0	0	10	10	5	10	10	10	68	8	100*
2	13	6	2	0	0	0	10	10	10	0	10	48	10	124
3	13	8	10	10	10	10	10	4	10	10	10	92	2	114
4	13	9	10	10	0	10	10	6	10	10	10	85	4	124
5	14	6	8	10	10	0	10	6	7	10	0	67	9	91
6	13	6	8	10	10	10	10	7	10	0	10	81	5	111
7	13	9	8	0	10	10	10	10	10	0	10	77	6	107
8	15	7	3	10	0	10	10	10	10	0	10	70	7	120*
9	13													
10	13	9	10	10	0	10	10	10	10	10	10	89	3	140
11	13	8	10	10	10	10	10	5	10	10	10	93	1	140*
12	14													

*Estimated

TABLE XVIII

Series II. Group C

Ind.	Age	1	2	3	4	5	6	7	8	9	10	G	R	IQ
1	15	4	3	0	10	0	0	10	8	10	10	55	7	100
2	14	6	5	10	10	10	0	8	10	10	10	79	3	95
3	15	7	10	10	10	10	10	10	4	10	10	91	1	111
4	13													
5	16	7	5	10	10	0	0	10	4	10	10	66	6	105
6	17	9	10	10	10	0	10	9	10	10	10	88	2	119
7	14													
8	16													
9	15	4	9	0	10	0	10	10	10	10	10	73	4	117
10	14													
11	15	8	5	10	10	0	0	9	7	10	10	69	5	124

See page 111 for key to captions.

TABLE XIX

Series II. Group E

Ind.	Age	1	2	3	4	5	6	7	8	9	10	G	R	IQ	Terman
1	13	6	7	10	10	0	0	7	10	0	10	60	11	136	117
2	13	4	3	10	0	0	0	10	10	0	10	47	13	91	82
3	12	8	10	10	10	0	10	7	10	10	10	85	3	119	105
4	13	4	7	10	10	0	10	10	10	0	0	61	10	78	
5	14	6	5	0	10	10	10	10	8	0	10	69	6	86	
6	13	7	8	10	10	10	0	10	8	0	10	78	4	115	
7	13	6	10	10	0	0	0	8	8	10	10	62	9	82	
8	14	10	10	10	0	10	10	10	10	10	10	90	1	111	
9	12	7	5	10	10	10	0	3	10	10	10	75	5	117	
10	10	6	3	10	0	0	0	5	10	0	10	44	14	123	
11	15	7	7	0	10	0	0	5	10	10	10	59	12	93	
12	12	7	10	10	0	0	0	8	10	10	10	65	7	139	
13	12	6	7	10	0	0	10	10	10	0	10	63	8	117	
14	17	6	10	10	10	10	0	10	10	10	10	86	2	69	

TABLE XX

Series II. Group I

Ind.	Age	1	2	3	4	5	6	7	8	9	10	G	R	IQ
1	12	4	0	0	10	0	0	5	10	0	0	29	5	109
2	12	3	0	0	10	0	0	7	8	0	0	28	6.5	97
3	11	7	7	10	10	0	0	7	10	0	10	61	3	141
4	11	6	0	10	10	0	0	7	10	0	0	43	4	100
5	11													100
6	12	1	5	0	10	0	0	5	7	0	0	28	6.5	115
7	12	9	10	10	10	0	0	10	10	10	10	79	1	61
8	11	5	5	10	10	0	0	8	10	10	10	68	2	101

See page 111 for key to captions.

TABLE XXI

Series II. Group J

Ind.	Age	1	2	3	4	5	6	7	8	9	10	M	G	R
1	12	6	10	10	10	0	0	0	10	0	10		56	
2	13	8	2	10	0	0	0	2	5	0	0		27	
3	12	8	2	10	10	10	0	10	10	7	10		77	
4	12	8	2	10	10	0	0	6	10	0	10		56	
5														
6	12	6	10	10	10	10	0	6	10	7	0		69	
7														
8	12	6	10	10	0	0	0	3	10	0	0		39	
9	12	8	10	10	10	0	0	10	10	7	0		65	
10	13	6	2	10	10	0	0	5	10	7	0		50	
11	12	6	10	10	0	10	0	2	10	0	0		48	

Average = 54

TABLE XXII

Series II. Group K

Ind.	Age	1	2	3	4	5	6	7	8	9	10	M	G	R
1	13	2	0	10	10	0	0	10	10	3	0		45	
2	12	2	0	0	10	0	0	5	10	0	0		27	
3	14	2	0	0	10	0	0	0	10	0	10		32	
4	13	6	0	10	10	0	0	5	10	3	0		44	
5	13	8	0	10	10	0	0	2	10	3	10		53	
6	14	8	0	10	10	0	0	2	10	8	10		58	
7	12	4	0	10	10	0	0	4	10	10	10		58	
8	13	4	0	0	10	0	0	10	10	7	10		51	
9														
10														
11	14	4	0	10	10	0	0	5	9	0	10		38	
12	14	0	8	0	10	0	0	8	10	0	0		36	

Average = 44.2

See page 111 for key to captions.

TABLE XXIII

COMPARING THE RESULTS OF THE TESTS OF GROUPS B, C, E, AND I IN PER CENTS

GROUP B. (*Experimental*)

$r = .21$

Subject	Series I	Series II	Change
1	68	68	0
2	66	48	—18
3	64	92	28
4	79	85	6
5	56	67	11
6	60	81	21
7	57	77	20
8	52	70	18
10	77	89	12
11	56	93	37
Totals	635	770	
Averages	63.5	77	+13.5

GROUP C. (*Experimental*)

$r = .56$

Subject	Series I	Series II	Change
1	23	55	32
2	76	79	3
3	55	91	36
5	67	66	—1
6	84	88	4
9	72	73	1
11	75	69	—6
Totals	452	521	
Averages	64.5	74.4	+9.9

TABLE XXIII—Continued

Group E. (Control Group)

$r = .63$

Subject	Series I	Series II	Change
1	65	60	— 5
2	43	47	4
3	80	85	5
4	67	61	— 6
5	77	69	— 8
6	67	78	11
7	78	62	—16
8	100	90	—10
9	88	75	—13
10	75	44	—31
11	63	59	— 4
12	88	65	—23
13	79	63	—16
14	80	86	6
Totals	1050	944	
Averages	75	67.4	—7.6

Group I. (Control Group)

$r = .85$

Subject	Series I	Series II	Change
1	53	29	—24
2	48	28	—20
3	52	61	9
4	41	43	2
6	33	28	— 5
7	95	79	—16
8	86	68	—18
Totals	408	336	
Averages	58.2	48	—10.2

TABLE XXIV

COMPARING THE RESULTS OF THE TESTS OF GROUPS J AND K IN PER CENTS

GROUP J

Subject	Series I	Series II	Change
1	23	56	33
2	24	27	3
3	57	77	20
4	36	56	20
6	36	69	33
8	46	39	—7
9	70	65	—5
10	38	50	12
11	22	48	26
Totals	352	487	
Averages	39.1	54.1	+15

GROUP K

Subject	Series I	Series II	Change
1	48	45	— 3
2	49	27	—22
3	42	32	—10
4	59	44	—15
5	80	53	—27
6	50	58	8
7	58	58	0
8	60	51	— 9
11	49	38	—11
12	49	36	—13
Totals	544	442	
Averages	54.4	44.2	—10.2

TABLE XXV

COMPARING THE RESULTS OF THE TWO SERIES OF TESTS IN RANKS

GROUP B. (*Experimental*)

Subject	Series I	Series II	Change
1	3	8	—5
2	4	10	—6
3	5	2	3
4	1	4	—3
5	8.5	9	— .5
6	6	5	1
7	7	6	1
8	10	7	3
10	2	3	—1
11	8.5	1	7.5

GROUP C. (*Experimental*)

Subject	Series I	Series II	Change
1	7	7	0
2	2	3	—1
3	6	1	5
5	5	6	—1
6	1	2	—1
9	4	4	0
11	3	5	—2

Group E. (Control Group)

Subject	Series I	Series II	Change
1	12	11	1
2	14	13	1
3	4.5	3	1.5
4	10.5	10	.5
5	8	6	—2
6	10.5	4	6.5
7	7	9	—2
8	1	1	0
9	2.5	5	—2.5
10	9	14	—5
11	13	12	1
12	2.5	7	—4.5
13	6	8	—2
14	4.5	2	2.5

Group I. (Control Group)

Subject	Series I	Series II	Change
1	3	5	—2
2	5	6.5	—1.5
3	4	3	1
4	6	4	2
6	7	6.5	.5
7	1	1	0
8	2	2	0

CHAPTER VI

CONCLUSIONS

There are a number of facts brought out in the experiment that seem to warrant the conclusion that ideals and attitudes perform an important function in the control of human conduct.

The first fact, as is seen from an inspection of Table XVI, shows that those groups which have been subjected to Scout training have a higher average of trustworthiness per individual than those groups which have not been thus subjected. Group H with two years of Scout training shows an average of 82 per cent in trustworthiness; Group D with six months of Scout training shows an average of 80 per cent. Two of the private school groups average 78 and 75 per cent respectively, but all of the other groups are lower.

The second fact, as is seen from an inspection of Table XXIII, is that the two experimental groups, B and C, show a marked improvement in trustworthiness between the first and the second series of tests. The average improvement in Group B was 13.5 per cent. The average improvement in Group C was 9.9 per cent. The control groups, on the contrary, average lower in the second series of tests than in the first. Group E averages 7.6 lower and Group I averages 10.2 lower in the second series of tests.

The lower averages of the control groups will not need to be taken as evidence that the control groups deteriorated between the time of the first and the second series of tests, but rather as evidence that the second series was more difficult. A comparison of the two series will convince the reader that this is the case. The actual average gain of the experimental groups, therefore, is greater than indicated by the scores of the second tests. It is as much greater as the amount of deterioration in the two control groups. Adding the average gains of the two experimental groups to the average losses of the two control groups gives a real difference in the gains of Groups B and C over Groups E and I of about 22 per cent. The unreliability of this difference, computed by the formula on page 193 of Thorndike's *Mental* and *Social Measurements*, is 3.016. (The unreliability is "the average deviation of the true difference minus the obtained difference. It represents a varying degree of probable approximation. This calculation is necessary because of the limited number of measurements. One more measurement, unless it happens to coincide with the average obtained, changes it.")

The question will be asked, how much of the 22 per cent gain is due to the general ideals resulting from scout training, and how much is due to the special training that was given to these two experimental groups? In order to ascertain, if possible, the superiority of the special methods which were used with these experimental groups, groups J and K were made subjects of additional experiment. Both of these groups had just been organized when the first series of the tests was given them. The leaders were not requested to give any special training; in fact, the leaders took no interest in the tests excepting to invite the boys to be present. About seven weeks of time elapsed between the first series of the tests and the second series. The results are given in Tables XIV, XV, XXI, XXII and XXIV.

Groups J and K did not have quite an equal chance with the experimental groups, B and C. Their period of training was somewhat shorter. Their leaders were probably less efficient, and the boys were much lower in the moral scale to begin with than any of the other groups that had been tested. Nevertheless, Group J showed an average improvement of 15 per cent. Group K showed a deterioration of 10.2 per cent. The difference between the two was doubtless due to the difference in the leadership. The leader of Group K was not even present at either of the tests. He showed very little interest in the boys. He delegated a friend of the scouts to visit the examiner at the time the tests were given in order to secure the payment of a dollar for each boy who was present at the tests. Nevertheless, his group of boys gave exactly the same results in the second series of tests as was shown by Group I, one of the control groups. The apparent falling off of 10.2 per cent probably does not mean a real falling off, but measures the difference in the difficulty of the tests of Series I and Series II.

The average of the boys of groups J and K for the tests of Series II was 47.2 per cent. The average of the same boys for the tests of Series II was 48.8 per cent. The average gain was 1.6 per cent. The inevitable conclusion is that general scout training, scattered as it is over a large field of idealism, does not bring the definite results that can be achieved when one ideal is emphasized, and that the leadership counts for very much more, perhaps, even than the methods of training.

The third fact, as may be seen from a further inspection of Table XXIII, shows that the correlation between the scores in the first and second series of tests is considerably higher in the control groups than in the experimental groups. This is evidence that the training took effect in the experimental groups, changing some individuals more than others and thus causing a general shifting in their rank in trustworthiness. Moreover, the higher correlation between the scores made in the two series in the control groups is evidence that the two series of tests measure the same thing.

One question that may be asked is whether there is reason to suppose that Groups B and C are by nature more likely to gain in trustworthiness than Groups E and I. Another question is whether Groups B and C might be more likely to discover the purpose of the tests than Groups E and I. and thus be on their guard. Both of these questions can be answered in large part by means of a comparison of the intelligence quotients of the individuals in the two sets of groups with their respective changes (gains or losses) in trustworthiness between the intervals of the two tests. The correlation between the per cent changes and the intelligence quotients of the individuals of Groups B and C is .14; and for Groups E and I, —.06. There is no reason to suppose, therefore, that the results were greatly affected by any difference in the intelligence of the two sets of groups.

There is considerable evidence of the improvement of the two experimental groups which it is impossible to put into cold figures. The boys improved in their manners, in cleanliness, in neatness, in their general deportment. The change was so marked in one of the two groups that a visitor who saw the troop shortly after its organization and again after a period of two months could hardly believe that they were the same boys.

During the tests there was evidence that the boys were being motivated by new ideals. "No, thank you; a Scout does not accept a tip for small favors." "It is no trouble; I do not want to be paid for it." "I am not going to cheat, even if I do not get the prize." "I did not earn this money; it would not be right for me to take it."

There is one fact which subtracts somewhat from the value of this experiment: some of the worst boys dropped out of the experimental groups. In Group B, individuals 9 and 12, who were ranked respectively 11 and 12 by the tests; and in Group C, individuals 4, 7, 8, and 10, who were ranked respectively 9, 6, 7, and 10 by the tests, failed to remain long in their troops.

The results of the experiment do not warrant the general conclusion that it is unnecessary to train children in the formation of specific habits of morality. In the first place, nothing was done with children under ten years of age. It is not likely that ideals exercise much control over conduct before that time. It would not be wise to leave the child untrained until such time as we may reasonably expect that ideals may be inculcated. In the second place, many of the habits which are formed early in life need to be carried on through later life. It would be a waste of time to postpone the formation of such habits until ideals have been established. In the third place, habits are mechanisms which may be put into the service of ideals, and the more of these there are convenient at hand, the more completely will ideals be able to control action.

It may be contended that this experiment is not sufficiently extended to permit of any valuable conclusions. Suppose that ideals can be taught within a space of two or three months and suppose that a group of boys will show much superior conduct at the end of the training period. This would not prove that at the end of three years the same boys will be at the level they have now attained. We would not expect them to be. Such assumptions are not made in arithmetic or spelling or music. A boy may attain a certain level of ability in arithmetic by the first of June, and when school opens in September he may show a profound ignorance of the subject. This fact does not discourage the teaching of arithmetic. For the same reason, it may be the part of wisdom to continue the teaching of ideals, even though their permanence can not be guaranteed. Undoubtedly ideals will deteriorate in the same way as any other mental attainment will deteriorate, by means of neglect and disuse. But once having been acquired, their relearning or revival would undoubtedly be easier than their first acquisition.

Thorndike says: "Morality is more susceptible than intellect to educational influences. Moral traits are more often matters of the direction of capacities and the creation of desires and aversions. Over them education has a greater sway, although school education, because of the narrow life of the school room, has so far done little for any save the semi-intellectual virtues." This statement is well borne out by the results of these tests. The actual amount of time given to the teaching of trustworthiness was very small. The troops met only once a week and the period of training lasted only 10 and 12 weeks respectively. The meetings were rarely more than two hours in length. Part of the time at each meeting was necessarily given over to routine and to such projects as are interesting to the boys. The teaching of trustworthiness was incidental. It probably consumed only a small fraction of the entire time of contact between the leaders and their boys. Nevertheless the results are much greater than would be expected from an equal expenditure of time and energy in the teaching of grammar or arithmetic.

One notable feature of the results is that the "good" boys show the least improvement. Individual 4 in Group B, who ranked 1 in the first series of tests, dropped down to fourth place in the second series, and showed an improvement of only six points. Individual 6 in Group C, who ranked 1 in the first series, dropped down to second place in the second series, and showed an improvement of only four points. Individuals 10, 1, and 2 in Group B, who ranked respectively 2, 3, and 4 in the first test, dropped down to third, eighth, and tenth places respectively in the second series of tests. In Group C, individuals 2, 11, and 9, who ranked respectively 2, 3, and 4 in the first series of tests, were third, fifth, and fourth respectively in the second series. On the other hand, many of the individuals who ranked low in the first series showed a remarkable improvement in the second series. It would seem as if the tendency of the groups is to level up the low places. Perhaps a longer period of training would show somewhat different results. But whether they would or not, the results of these tests show a decided tendency toward negative acceleration on the part of those who stood nearest the top.

It was not to be expected of course that uniform results would be achieved even with uniform treatment. We do not get such results in our teaching of arithmetic or spelling or music. Some individuals who are subjected to training have already approximated their limit of improvement. Moreover, in the field of moral training, as in other fields, individual differences in native capacity will stare us in the face. It is doubtless true that some individuals could never be made as trustworthy as other individuals, no matter how much training is given. When the upper limits are approached, intelligence will doubtless play a very important part. Nevertheless it is probably true that it is easier to equalize individuals in morality than in intelligence. In moral education, it is extremely likely that an increased amount of training will decrease differences instead of increasing them, as is the case in intellectual education.

However, it is probably true that the highest and finest ideals can be acquired only by those who are superior in intelligence. In the field of moral education, as in other fields, it is necessary to use the material which we find. The effective teacher of trustworthiness or of any other moral trait is the one who can establish the greatest number or the strongest bonds between certain situations and the desired responses. But he will not be satisfied with the creation of specific bonds only. He will create, if possible, a tendency to act in accordance with certain general concepts for which an emotional appreciation has been established in the mind of each individual.

Civic, moral, and religious education will need to emphasize the inculcation of right ideals. Without such ideals all social education will drop to the level of trick training. These ideals must be so reinforced by means of emotional experiences that they will be able to inhibit the response of habits that are contrary to their purpose, and to regulate the response of habits which are in harmony with their purpose. With faith in the function of these ideals and of the attitudes which are generated by them, it will be possible to build broad and comprehensive programs of social education; and the men of faith, who are pouring out their treasure and their lives in such efforts as BOY SCOUTING and the

Interchurch World Movement, may hope to be rewarded for their efforts by the gradual raising of the standards of citizenship in the growing generation, and in the gradual realization of the dream of a real Democracy.

THE FUNCTION OF IDEALS
IN SOCIAL EDUCATION

PAUL F. VOELKER

COLUMBIA UNIVERSITY
CONTRIBUTIONS TO EDUCATION
TEACHERS COLLEGE SERIES